IMAGES
of America

CYPRESS HILLS
CEMETERY

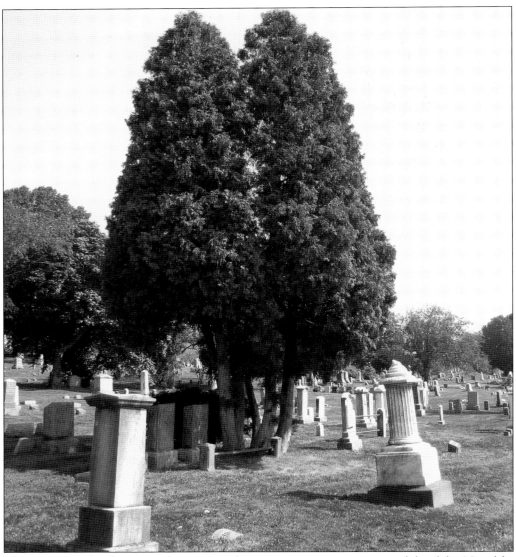

The cypress tree has been a staple ornament for centuries in cemeteries around the globe. Noted for its balsamic fragrance, this slow growing tree is renowned for its longevity and serves as a symbol of immortality for many cultures. As the cypress tree endures, so does Cypress Hills Cemetery. Established 38 years before the unveiling of the Statue of Liberty (1886), this quiet place of peaceful repose has proudly, and with dignity, served the needs of the surrounding community and that of the city of New York as a whole for the past 162 years. (Authors' collection.)

ON THE COVER: The original main entrance to Cypress Hills Cemetery was a formal classical wooden structure with a high central archway. The heavy wooden gates were hung on metal hinges as a sign of the industrial age. The high fence with ornate finials enclosed the entire cemetery property. Well-dressed family and friends pose for a moment in the hot sun while waiting for a funeral procession to arrive. This entranceway was replaced by a stone archway under a peaked roof in 1893. This dated image goes as far back as the late 1870s. (Courtesy of Cypress Hills Cemetery Archives.)

IMAGES
of America

CYPRESS HILLS
CEMETERY

Stephen C. Duer and Allan B. Smith

ARCADIA
PUBLISHING

Published by Arcadia Publishing
Charleston, South Carolina

Printed in the United States of America

Library of Congress Control Number: 2010921765

For all general information contact Arcadia Publishing at:
Telephone 843-853-2070
Fax 843-853-0044
E-mail sales@arcadiapublishing.com
For customer service and orders:
Toll-Free 1-888-313-2665

Visit us on the Internet at www.arcadiapublishing.com

*Dedicated in memory of my parents, Kathryn and Francis Smith,
who taught me to honor, respect, and appreciate cemeteries.*

—Allan Smith

*Dedicated to my wife, Christina, and my three children, Emily Rose,
Stevie, and Andy, who were extremely supportive and patient with me.*

—Stephen Duer

Contents

ACKNOWLEDGMENTS

In crafting this book our goals were to accurately depict a historic treasure filled with an engaging past, aesthetic beauty, and notable New Yorkers that came before us. During this process we have met individuals that have been a tremendous help in making this project come to fruition. The authors wish to give special acknowledgment and thanks to William E. Moloney, the office manager of Cypress Hills Cemetery, for his utmost support and dedication. In addition, we thank the following Cypress Hills Cemetery officers for their cooperation: John Desmond, president; Mario Gil, vice president; Anthony Russo, superintendent; Patrick Russo, family service counselor; and Anthony Desmond, foreman. Thank you also to the following cemetery staff: Mirella Marte, Lori Tagle, Mary Cordon, Valerie Young, and Carolina Padin. We acknowledge Judith May and Elizabeth Call of the Brooklyn Historical Society as well as the archives team of John Hyslop, Eric Huber, and Ian Lewis at the Queens Borough Public Library for their contributions. We also recognize the following: Kurt T. Kraska, author of *The History of Cypress Hills Cemetery and Its Permanent Residents*; Tricia Foley of Yaphank Historical Society; Albert W. O'Leary of the New York City Police Benevolent Society; Robert Dickert of Great Uncle Peter's Steakhouse; Nicole Bates of Delta Sigma Theta Sorority; and Joe Fodor. Unless otherwise noted, all photographs are from the authors' collection. Finally, a sincere gesture of appreciation goes to Erin Vosgien, junior publisher at Arcadia Publishing, for her patience and professional guidance.

INTRODUCTION

The 19th century brought great changes to New York City. The city was leaving its colonial past behind and expanding rapidly. This growth influenced the emergence of an industrial revolution that attracted more people to the city, which ultimately resulted in the need for more burial space.

In 1813, churchyard space became increasingly scarce, and Manhattan forefathers confronted this issue by forbidding any internments below Canal Street. By 1851, this border had been pushed uptown as far as Eighty-sixth Street and forced the civic leaders in these progressive communities to explore other options. The idea that rural territories, far removed from the turmoil and encroachments of the city, could be converted into picturesque permanent burial grounds, separate from any church and exclusively for that purpose, became an attractive solution to this ever-increasing problem. The "rural cemetery" movement had begun, and its Brooklyn exponents were the founders of Cypress Hills Cemetery.

The Rural Cemetery Act, which became law on April 27, 1847, authorized burials to become a commercial business to be pursued outside the city limits for the first time in American history. One year and seven months later, on November 21, 1848, Cypress Hills Cemetery was dedicated. This was the first cemetery in Greater New York to be organized under this law, which has been internationally recognized as "America's contribution to the civilized burial of the dead."

The land before it became Cypress Hills Cemetery was originally part of the Thomas Betts farm, which straddled the Kings and Queens County line. The Van Wycks, who were the owners of this farm after 1836, sold the acreage to the cemetery founders for $25,000. These poignant visionaries all realized the need for a modern and endowed cemetery for Brooklyn where plot costs would exclude no one. They adopted the most progressive principles and regulations for the protection of the plot owners, and they instituted an endowment system that ensured the perpetuity of the facility. The founders of Cypress Hills were planning the cemetery of tomorrow. So it was with courage and vision that they "looked up into the hills" instead of the lowlands, where the land was available at less cost. They searched for a location where richly wooded hills and dells were dotted with lakes and ponds, as they sought to attain the seclusion, privacy, and pensive tranquility of the ideal rural cemetery. The land that the founders selected was elevated, which provided commanding vistas of Jamaica Bay and the ocean beyond. The founders believed that the union of beauty and nature would benefit both the living and the dead. The landscape designers and groundskeepers engaged in laborious grading, filling, and road building, all of which was done without the benefit of steam shovels or industrial equipment, but with strong hands and horses.

The first interment, David Fay Corey, occurred on December 11, 1848. This officially established the cemetery as a tax-exempt burial ground, and it opened to the public in 1851. Nine short years after the first burial, there were 35,257 interments made at Cypress Hills. Reinterments from old cemeteries in Manhattan became a daily occurrence, and five Methodist churches alone removed approximately 14,000 of their dead and reinterred them at Cypress Hills.

The beauty of the cemetery and the egalitarian principles that governed its operation soon attracted the attention of many religious, fraternal, and benevolent organizations. This "fellowship in immortality" was encouraged by the founders: "It is our ambition and our hope to see all religious denominations, orders of benevolence, and national and industrial societies meet together on this common ground, and by proximity and goodwill, acknowledge that all men are brethren, having a common origin and a common destiny." A few such organizations included the Metropolitan Police Benevolent Burial Association, the Journalistic Fraternity, and the American Dramatist Fund. Cypress Hill's permanent residents are as diverse as New York City itself.

It is the final resting place of actors, athletes, politicians, activists, eccentrics, authors, artists, musicians, and notorious organized-crime figures. Many early Brooklyn residents repose here, such as Otto Huber, founder of the Huber Brewing empire; Robert Ferguson, a much-admired baseball player nicknamed "Death to Flying Objects"; Peter Luger, founder of the nationally acclaimed steak house in Williamsburg; and the first families of Brooklyn whose names are immortalized on street signs, such as Pitkin, Eldert, Cozine, and Wyckoff. The cemetery also reflects the tragedies of big-city life. This is exemplified in the graves of seven-year-old Nixmary Brown, a tragic abuse case, and eight-year-old Gavin Cato, an accident victim who died on a Brooklyn sidewalk, igniting the Crown Heights riots. Cypress Hills Cemetery is also the final resting place for the parents of Ben Vereen, the father of Tony Danza, and the mother of Hollywood icon Burt Lancaster. In fiction, Marvel Comics has used Cypress Hills as the headquarters of the superhero team the Midnight Suns and the burial location for Peter Parker's parents in *Spider-Man* lore.

Cypress Hills is also steeped in ethnic diversity, for the number of ethnic cultures that lie in repose inside the grounds is astonishing. Large Chinese sections lie next to Greek, Spanish, Albanian, Jewish, Japanese, and German areas.

Cypress Hills Cemetery holds the distinction of being home to a U.S. National Cemetery. Established in 1862, this 3.5-acre area became the precursor of the larger Cypress Hills National Cemetery located farther west on Jamaica Avenue. Inside this sacred ground are the men who served gallantly for our freedoms. One such notable group was the Michigan Iron Brigade, considered to be one of the finest troops in the Union army. Also situated inside the cemetery grounds is the Mount of Victory plot, the final resting place of men who served in the War of 1812, which includes the oldest living veteran of that war, Hiram Cronk. Scattered about the cemetery grounds today are the remains of eight Medal of Honor recipients.

Since its inception, Cypress Hills has interred approximately 380,000. Presently, the cemetery buries at least five to six deceased per day, which makes it one of the busiest cemeteries in Greater New York. The grand vision of the facility is to strike a sensitive balance in the preservation of the historic portions, while continuing to serve the community by providing new burial space for years to come. Fortunately for the public, the officials and trustees of Cypress Hills have never deviated from the ideals of its founders. In these days of continuous change, it is heartening to know that institutions like Cypress Hills can honor and respect tradition and ideals. During times of great prosperity or of deep depression, Cypress Hills maintains the even tenor of its way.

For the benefit of many who manage their way through life by toil and thrift, tribute should be paid to Cypress Hills for traditionally meeting the needs and the circumstances of the average American family. Ostentation, extravagant displays of wealth, and commercialism have been scrupulously avoided. The sentiment and sorrow of a humble family commands precisely the same respect and attention accorded to the rich, and this has become the treasured hallmark of Cypress Hills Cemetery.

One

INCEPTION AND
DEVELOPMENT

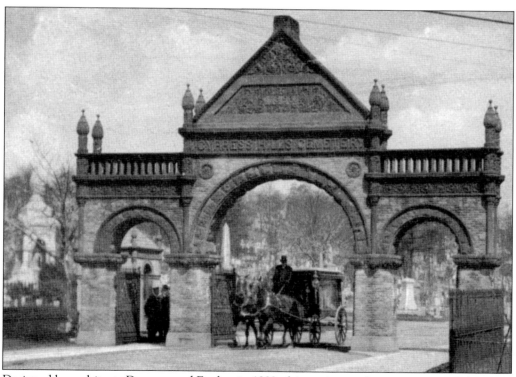

Designed by architects Danmar and Fischer in 1893, this ancient archway once graced the main entrance of Cypress Hills Cemetery. Constructed of Longmeadow brownstone and pressed brick, the side archways were 5 feet wide and the central arch was 12 feet wide. Notice the distinguished driver in a top hat as he leaves the cemetery grounds. Unfortunately, this handsome historical archway no longer exists. (Courtesy of Cypress Hills Cemetery Archives.)

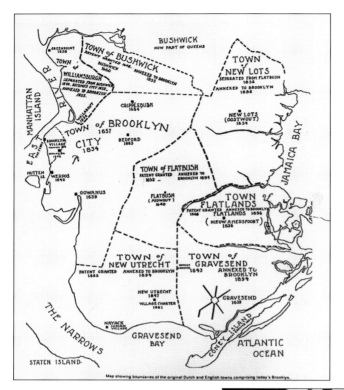

Map showing boundaries of the original Dutch and English towns comprising today's Brooklyn.

Over the years, the Dutch settlers created five towns: Brooklyn, Flatlands, Flatbush, New Utrecht, and Bushwick. English settlers created Gravesend, a sixth town. The town of New Lots, which included Cypress Hills Cemetery, separated from the town of Flatbush (Old Lots) in 1852 and encompassed the small rural villages of Cypress Hills, East New York, and Brownsville. (Courtesy of Brooklyn Historical Society.)

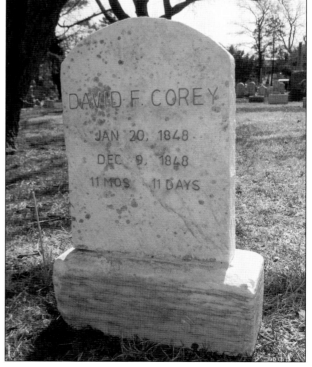

David F. Corey holds the distinction of being the first person interred in Cypress Hills Cemetery. Young David only lived for 11 months and 11 days, dying of a respiratory infection, a common illness during the mid-1800s. Located in Section 1, Corey was buried on December 11, 1848, setting the stage for over 380,000 interments to follow.

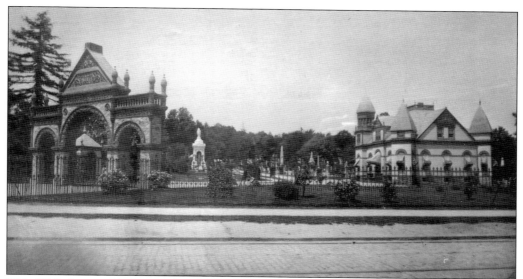

This 1915 photograph depicts the administration building in its original style. Framed in wood, the building was originally clad in white with brownstone trim, including a beehive turret. The main entrance, adorned with a Victorian arch, complemented the administration building upon entering. To the right of the arch is the prominent Otto Huber family plot. At the bottom of the photograph, Jamaica Avenue is shown with trolley tracks running through the cobblestones. (Courtesy of Cypress Hills Cemetery Archives.)

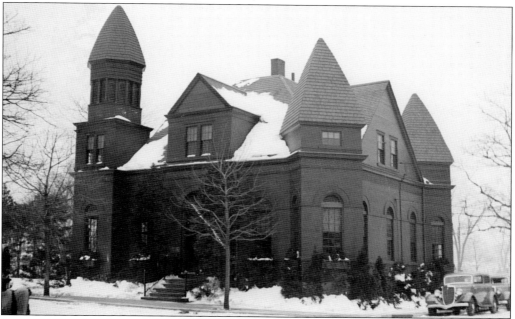

In the 1930s, the administration building was completely repainted either brown or dark red, which gave the structure a much more somber appearance. Located at the main entrance, the administration building is where all business activities and burial arrangements are conducted. This Victorian-style building was razed in the 1960s and today is the site of a modern two-story administration building. (Courtesy of Cypress Hills Cemetery Archives.)

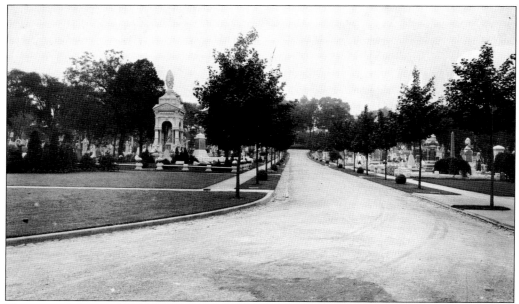

This main cemetery thoroughfare that welcomes visitors into the grounds is named Via Dolorosa. Many of the headstones and monuments situated on both sides of this tree-lined road are some of the oldest stones to be found in Cypress Hills. The elaborate Huber monument at left was placed there in 1890. At the end of this roadway in the distant hillside was the receiving tomb. (Courtesy of Cypress Hills Cemetery Archives.)

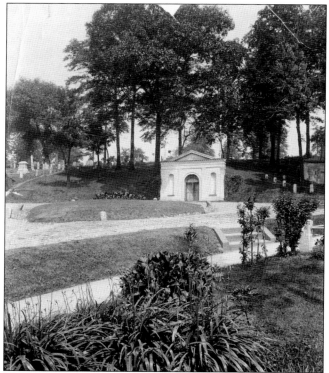

Via Dolorosa leads up to the once-existing receiving tomb. This structure was utilized to temporarily store bodies when harsh weather, frozen ground, plot ownership, and interment delays impeded burial. The receiving tomb contained numerous crypts. In addition to the removal of the receiving tomb, the steps and the sidewalk have been reconfigured to accommodate more grave space. (Courtesy of Cypress Hills Cemetery Archives.)

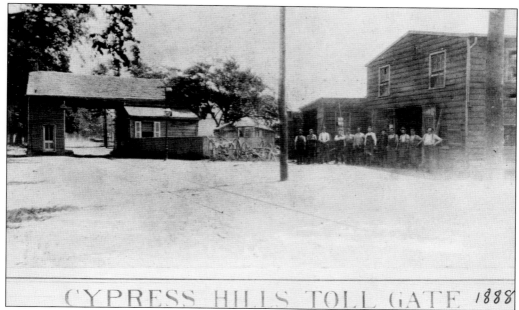

CYPRESS HILLS TOLL GATE 1888

The Jamaica Plank Road ran from Williamsburgh in Brooklyn to the Village of Jamaica in Queens. Stagecoaches, and later horse-drawn trolleys, ran along this route, which was the southernmost boundary of the cemetery. The road had wooden planks laid on it to facilitate travel when inclement weather would wash away the earthen surface, hence the name Jamaica Plank Road. The road had three tollgates, one of which was located at Nichols Avenue near the entrance to Cypress Hills Cemetery. (Courtesy of Brooklyn Historical Society.)

Usually brownstone headstones are seen in private family burial grounds, and if seen in Cypress Hills Cemetery, this indicates that they were removed from older private cemeteries or from churchyards in Manhattan. The date of death on this weathered stone is 1805, proving that it is older than Cypress Hills Cemetery, which opened in 1848.

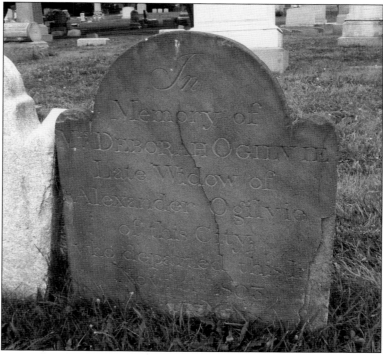

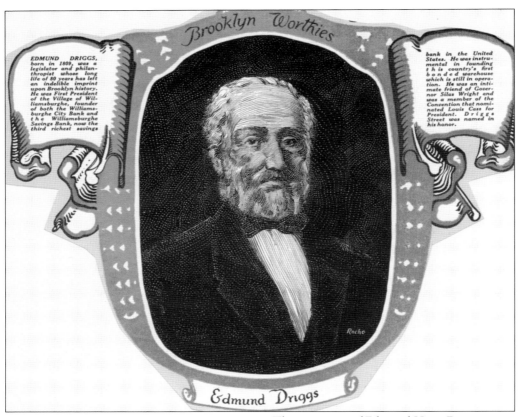

EDMUND DRIGGS, born in 1809, was a legislator and philanthropist whose long life of 80 years has left an indelible imprint upon Brooklyn history. He was First President of the Village of Williamsburghe, founder of both the Williamsburghe City Bank and the Williamsburghe Savings Bank, now the third richest savings

bank in the United States. He was instrumental in founding this country's first bonded warehouse which is still in operation. He was an intimate friend of Governor Silas Wright and was a member of the Convention that nominated Louis Cass for President. Driggs Street was named in his honor.

Roche

Edmund Driggs

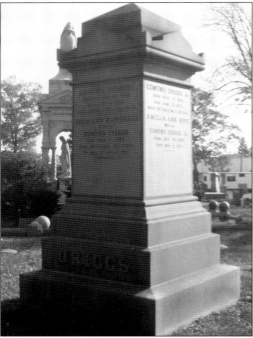

The grave site of Edmund Hope Driggs (1865–1946) is located in Section 1. Driggs was a prominent and well-known businessman, politician, and Cypress Hills Cemetery president. He held many prominent office positions, including president of the Village of Williamsburg in 1850. By the mid-1850s, he became a trustee and vice president of Cypress Hills Cemetery. He helped organize the Williamsburg City Fire Insurance Company. In 1860, Driggs became president of the Grand Street Newton Railroad Company, and in 1878, he was appointed president of Cypress Hills Cemetery, where he diligently served the burial needs of the local community for over 20 years. In 1896, he entered into politics and was elected as a congressman, serving until 1901. Congressman Driggs died of pneumonia at age 81. (Above, courtesy of Brooklyn Historical Society; left, authors' collection.)

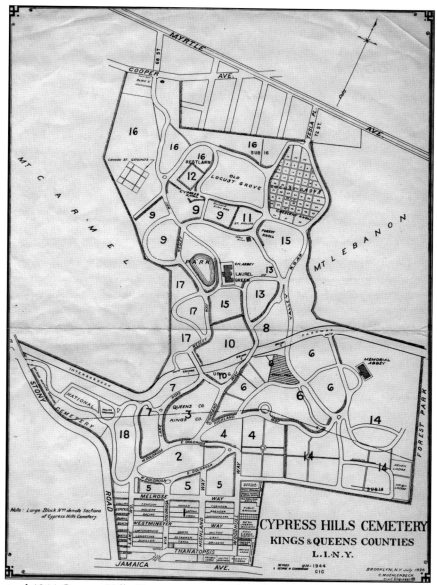

This revised 1944 Cypress Hills Cemetery map displays the grounds of the 209-acre facility. The horizontal line toward the bottom of the map indicates the boundary of Kings and Queens Counties. It is safe to assume that there are people buried on or around this line whose bodies would then be in two different counties. Even though the majority of the land is in Queens, the main entrance and office is in Brooklyn, making it officially a Brooklyn-based cemetery. Shown are two buildings—the Cypress Hills Abbey, located by a lake, and the Memorial Abbey. Both are located in Queens. The rolling topography of the property near the Interboro Parkway lends itself to winding picturesque roadways. There are over 40 miles of roads and paths, many named after classical English writers. The flatter southern portion of the property is laid out in a more formal grid pattern. The original Cypress Hills National Cemetery is at the far left of the map off Stoney Road. Cypress Hills Cemetery itself is sandwiched between Mount Lebanon and Mount Carmel, the two neighboring Jewish cemeteries. (Courtesy of Cypress Hills Cemetery Archives.)

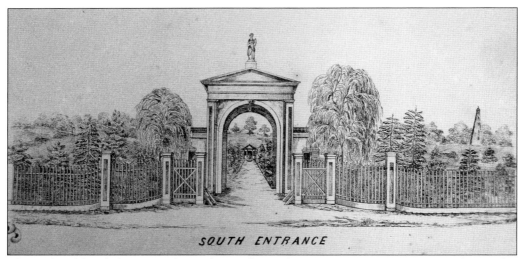

SOUTH ENTRANCE

This undated detailed artist rendering depicts the south entrance on Jamaica Avenue. The wooden arched entranceway is flanked by two weeping willow trees, symbolic of sadness and mourning. In the distance under the arch, the receiving tomb is illustrated. The wooden observation tower, at far right, was a popular attraction at the cemetery during the 19th century. None of these structures, including the trees, exist today. (Courtesy of Queens Public Library.)

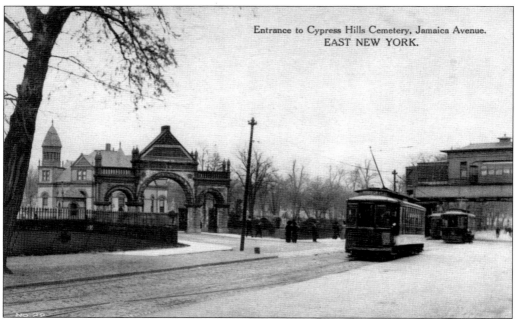

Entrance to Cypress Hills Cemetery, Jamaica Avenue.
EAST NEW YORK.

This c. 1910 image depicts the Cypress Hills Cemetery entrance and the administration building. The newly paved Jamaica Avenue is equipped with trolley tracks, which remain in the hand-laid cobblestones. At right is the Cypress Hills station of the Brooklyn-Manhattan Transit (BMT) elevated line. Years later, the elevated line was extended along Jamaica Avenue to reach the steadily growing Jamaica business district. This elevated line continues to serve the transportation needs of New Yorkers today. (Courtesy of Brooklyn Historical Society.)

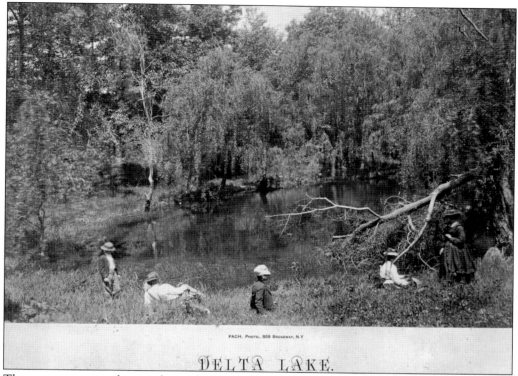

PACH, PHOTO., 858 BROADWAY, N.Y

DELTA LAKE.

The cemetery grounds were forested with many specimen trees, including willow trees, which thrive near bodies of water or in areas with a high water table that feeds its roots. It was not uncommon for families to visit the cemetery, especially on weekends, to picnic on the grounds and to enjoy a day in the country. Originally there were 13 small lakes and ponds on the cemetery property. They have all since been filled in to make room for future graves. (Courtesy of Cypress Hills Cemetery Archives.)

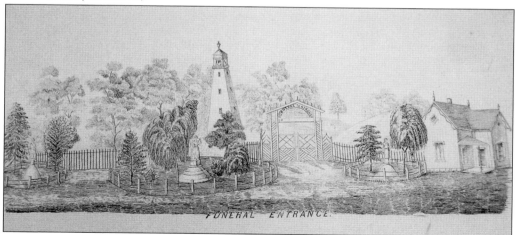

FUNERAL ENTRANCE.

At the western end of the cemetery off the Williamsburgh Macadamized Road stood the funeral entrance, where three stone statues greeted the new arrivals. Inside the gate, a wooden tower that contained a bell was rung to alert cemetery workers of the funeral procession. This entrance and tower no longer exist. (Courtesy of Queens Public Library.)

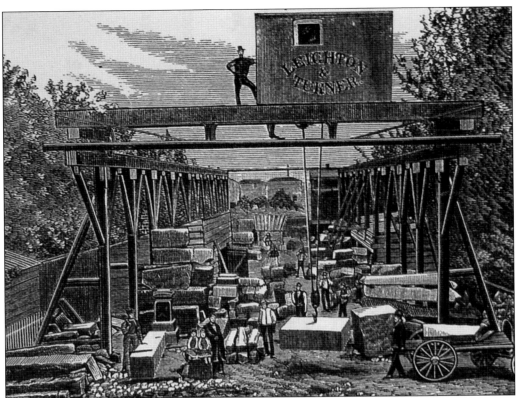

Cypress Hills Cemetery spurred much business along Jamaica Avenue. Many stone yards, monument makers and sellers, as well as florists were established opposite the cemetery's main entrance. Leighton and Turner, located on Jamaica Avenue near Crescent Street, was one of the most successful monument makers in the area. Their large sheds were used for cutting and sculpting heavy blocks of marble and granite. The detailed lithograph above shows the stone yard in action, which includes two children sitting with their mother beside them, suggesting a family-owned business. Considering the time, full-page advertisements like the one below were a very expensive way to advertise one's business. (Above, courtesy of Cypress Hills Cemetery Archives; below, courtesy of Queens Public Library.)

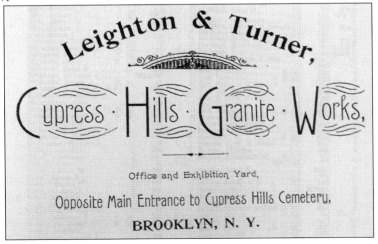

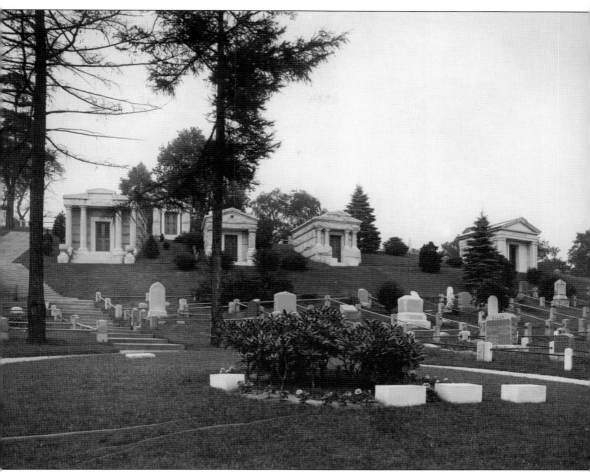

Taking advantage of the steep topography, many stately mausoleums were built into the hillsides. Located in Section 14, these building sites were some of the most expensive plots to purchase because they offered spectacular views of Cypress Hills and beyond to Jamaica Bay. The mausoleum at far right belongs to William Miles, a former long-serving president of Cypress Hills Cemetery. The neighboring wide steps, seen at left above, lead up to a winding roadway called William Miles Way, named in his honor. The more gentle slopes afforded burial sites for family plots, many enclosed with low railings. Evergreen trees abounded with shrubbery, perennials, and annual flowers beautifying the grounds. The term "mausoleum" is derived from King Mausolus (died 353 BCE), a governor of Caria in ancient Persia, who had a large stately tomb built for himself. (Courtesy of Cypress Hills Cemetery Archives.)

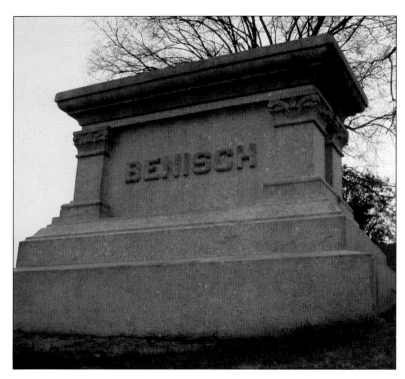

The Benisch brothers owned and operated a monument and stonecutting establishment on Jamaica Avenue that serviced Cypress Hills. Large sheds, overhead rails with moving pulleys, and saws for cutting large blocks of stone made up the Benisch brothers' busy stone yard. The family headstone is situated on a steep hillside facing east in the general direction of the Benisch Stone Works. The company is no longer in business.

This rendering of an early Cypress Hills plot map included ornamental gardens that lined the main entrance road. Above the receiving tomb is the Mount of Victory plot. Paths in this area are named after significant battle sites such as Bunker Hill and Saratoga. Paths in the lower section are named after classic writers, dramatists, and poets. The penmanship, detail, and overall illustration are to be admired. (Courtesy of Queens Public Library.)

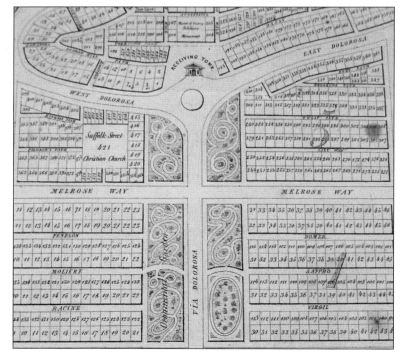

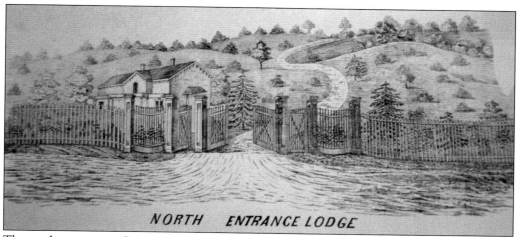

NORTH ENTRANCE LODGE

The north entrance or Cooper Avenue gate in Glendale was originally designed to include a visitors' lodge. The lodge was intended to accommodate weary visitors who spent long hours traveling from the city to visit the cemetery; however, it was not to be used for overnight stays. The swing gate, wooden fence, lodge, and the rolling tree-filled hills are an artist's conception. According to cemetery records, the lodge was never constructed. (Courtesy of Queens Public Library.)

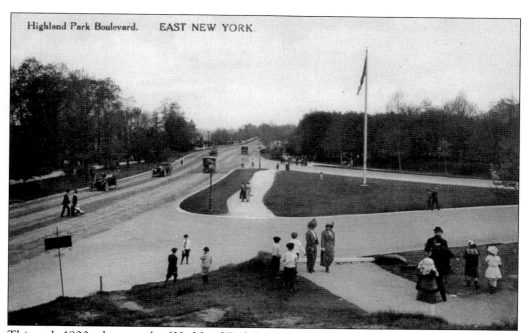

Highland Park Boulevard.   EAST NEW YORK.

This early-1900s photograph of Highland Park Boulevard gives us a window into a typical Sunday in the neighborhood. The two-way main street runs along the high ridge where Cypress Hills Cemetery is located. Notice the locals in their Sunday best as they stroll toward Highland Park, home to the Ridgewood Reservoir. Today the western end of the street is lined with stately mansions. (Courtesy of Brooklyn Historical Society.)

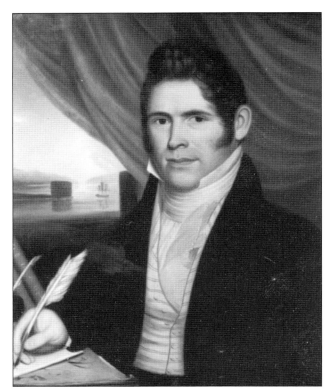

Born into a prominent Connecticut family, John R. Pitkin (1794–1847) came to New York at a young age and worked in the dry goods trade. In 1816, he began buying up, one by one, the farms in what eventually became East New York, Brooklyn, from the old Dutch farmers. By the mid-1830s he had amassed a comfortable fortune, and in 1835, he purchased the land in what is now Woodhaven. On a hillside, Pitkin rests under this imposing monument alongside his wife, Sophia M. Thrall Pitkin, who died on November 30, 1849. Appropriately, the plot sits high on a hill in Section 4 looking out over the land that he developed and loved so much. (Left, courtesy of Brooklyn Historical Society; below, authors' collection.)

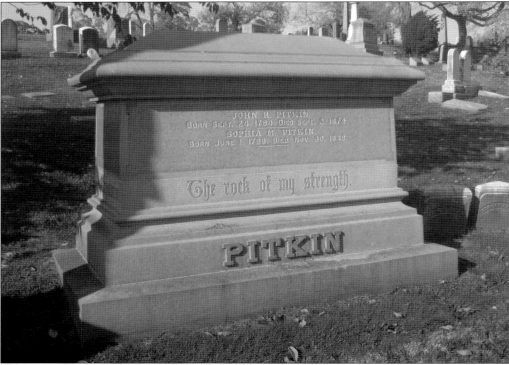

JOHN R. PITKIN
BORN SEPT. 24, 1794. DIED SEPT. 2, 1874.
SOPHIA M. PITKIN
BORN JUNE 1, 1798. DIED NOV. 30, 1849.

The rock of my strength.

PITKIN

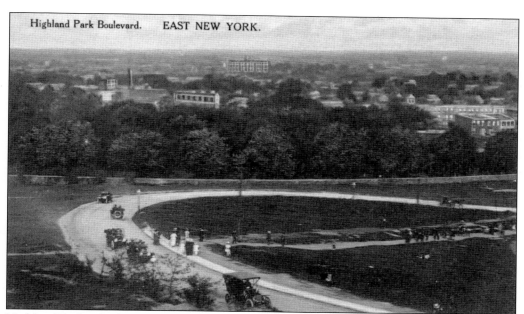

Highland Park, which opened in 1913, contains 141 acres. The park is located west of Cypress Hills Cemetery along Jamaica Plank Road. The trees in the background are in Cypress Hills National Cemetery. The village of Cypress Hills is located in the upper portion of this image. At far right, a horse-drawn carriage is amidst the "horseless carriages." (Courtesy of Brooklyn Historical Society.)

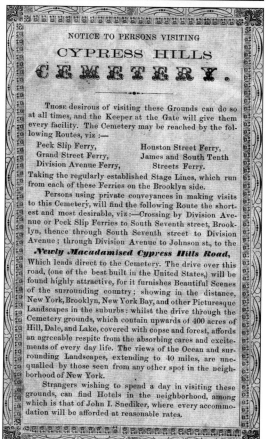

NOTICE TO PERSONS VISITING

CYPRESS HILLS CEMETERY.

THOSE desirous of visiting these Grounds can do so at all times, and the Keeper at the Gate will give them every facility. The Cemetery may be reached by the following Routes, viz:—

Peck Slip Ferry,   Houston Street Ferry,
Grand Street Ferry,   James and South Tenth
Division Avenue Ferry,   Streets Ferry.

Taking the regularly established Stage Lines, which run from each of these Ferries on the Brooklyn side.

Persons using private conveyances in making visits to this Cemetery, will find the following Route the shortest and most desirable, viz:—Crossing by Division Avenue or Peck Slip Ferries to South Seventh street, Brooklyn, thence through South Seventh street to Division Avenue; through Division Avenue to Johnson st., to the

Newly Macadamised Cypress Hills Road,

Which leads direct to the Cemetery. The drive over this road, (one of the best built in the United States,) will be found highly attractive, for it furnishes Beautiful Scenes of the surrounding country; showing in the distance, New York, Brooklyn, New York Bay, and other Picturesque Landscapes in the suburbs: whilst the drive through the Cemetery grounds, which contain upwards of 400 acres of Hill, Dale, and Lake, covered with copse and forest, affords an agreeable respite from the absorbing cares and excitements of every day life. The views of the Ocean and surrounding Landscapes, extending to 40 miles, are unequalled by those seen from any other spot in the neighborhood of New York.

Strangers wishing to spend a day in visiting these grounds, can find Hotels in the neighborhood, among which is that of John I. Snediker, where every accommodation will be afforded at reasonable rates.

The back page of a late-1800s Cypress Hills Cemetery catalogue lists the various means of transportation available to reach the cemetery. Those desirous of visiting could use ferries traveling across from lower Manhattan and then connect with stagecoach lines, or they could come on their own using the newly paved macadamized road. Take note at the bottom that the John Snediker Roadhouse is recommended for local lodging. (Courtesy of Cypress Hills Cemetery Archives.)

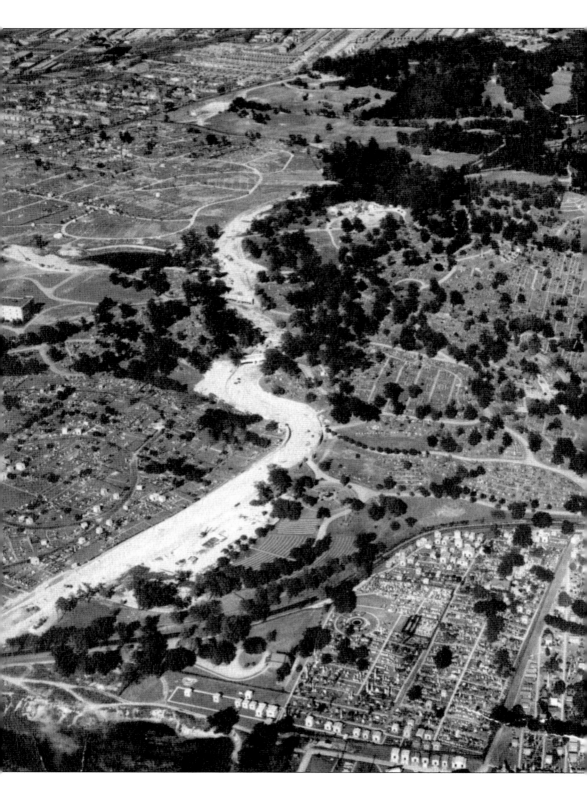

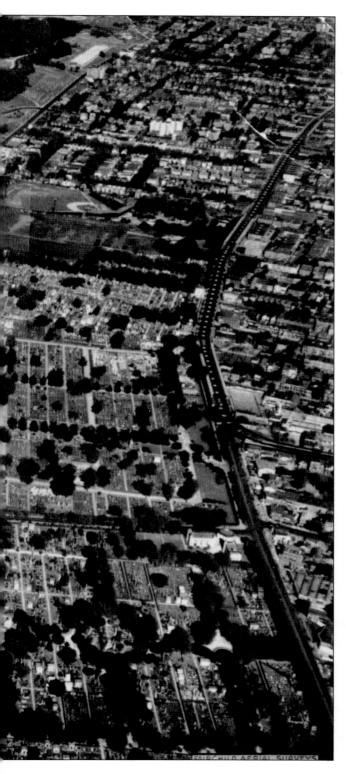

FAIRCHILD AERIAL SURVEYS

This vintage 1931 photograph taken by Fairchild Aerial Surveys, Inc., shows the entire 209-acre Cypress Hills Cemetery. The broad curving white band on the left indicates the ongoing construction of the Interboro Parkway. To the right of the roadway, notice the small straight white lines that are the headstones of war veterans, which are located in the national cemetery section of Cypress Hills. The dense forested area at the top of the photograph is Forest Park, the third largest park in Queens County. The building located on the extreme left is the Cypress Hills Abbey, which is the largest structure in the photograph. On the upper right, take notice of the baseball field; this was Dexter Park, a minor league ballpark where Babe Ruth once played. Two-family attached brick housing has since replaced the ballpark. (Courtesy of Cypress Hills Cemetery Archives.)

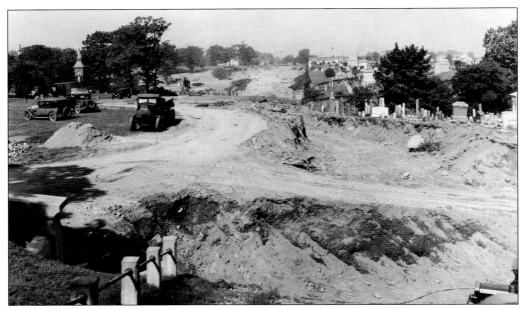

These 1931 construction photographs of the Interboro Parkway show the intended route cutting directly through the sacred grounds of Cypress Hills Cemetery. This was clearly, without question, the biggest challenge the engineers had to face during the parkway's construction. The goal was to relocate as few existing graves sites as possible, and as a result, the parkway twists and turns throughout the cemetery grounds. With family permission and compensation, many bodies were disinterred and reburied in other locations. Welsh Brothers was the general contractor for the project. In the top photograph, above the classic cars, is the Henry W. Meyer monument. On the far left, below the dirt road, notice the corner of a hillside mausoleum, while headstones await removal near the bottom. In the below photograph looking east, a supervisor oversees the operation. (Courtesy of Cypress Hills Cemetery Archives.)

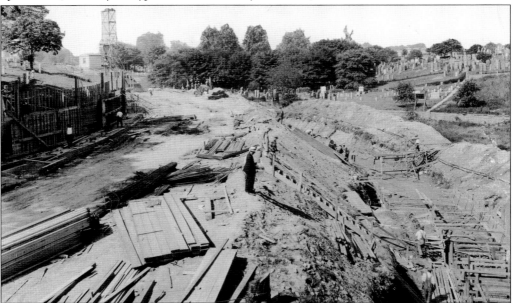

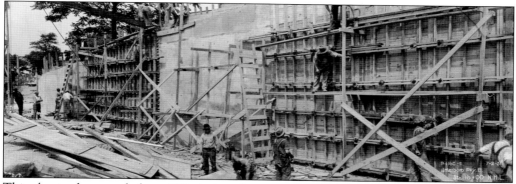

This classic photograph from 1931 depicts the ongoing construction of the retaining walls of the Interboro Parkway. The intricate wooden framework, essential for concrete pouring, shores up both sides of the roadway. Built during the Depression, the contractor paid most men a daily wage, just enough to feed the family. Predating Occupational Safety and Health Administration (OSHA) laws, safety was not of the upmost concern. This is reflected in the workers not wearing hard hats or safety straps. (Courtesy of Cypress Hills Cemetery Archives.)

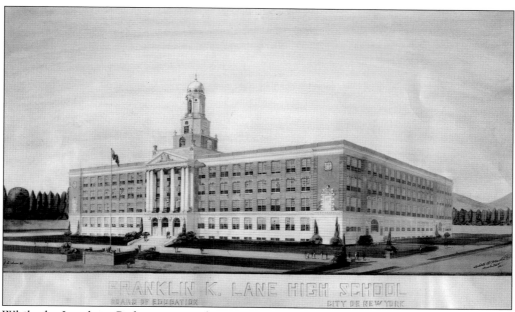

While the Interboro Parkway was under construction, Franklin K. Lane High School was also being built. Franklin K. Lane is named for Woodrow Wilson's interior secretary, who is best remembered for introducing the National Park Services in 1916. When completed at a cost of over $3 million, the school could accommodate 5,100 students, making it the largest academic high school in the world. Situated on Jamaica Avenue and Dexter Court, the school is east of the main cemetery entrance. (Courtesy of Brooklyn Historical Society.)

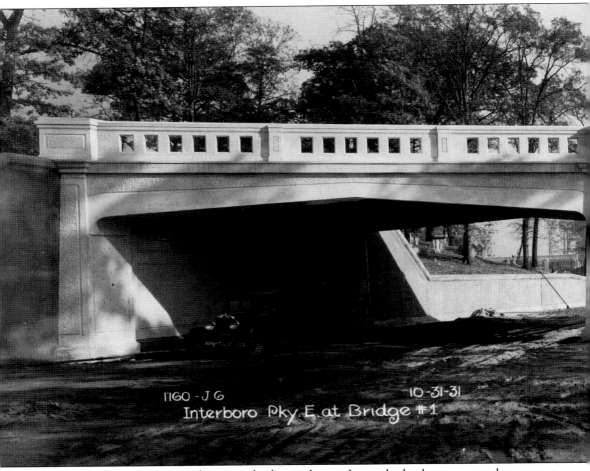

1160 - J 6   10-31-31
Interboro Pky. E. at Bridge #1

Bisected by the Interboro Parkway, two bridges and an underpass had to be constructed to connect both the north and south sides of the Cypress Hills Cemetery. This 1931 image shows the completed West Bridge, while under the left archway the East Bridge can be seem. The double-span overpass was constructed of textured concrete; each span formed a slightly pointed arch opening. Under the

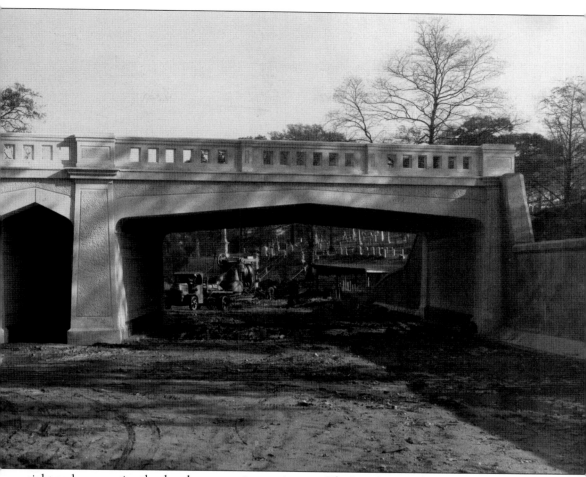

right archway, notice the dated construction equipment. The Interboro Parkway was designed for automobile traffic only. The 73-year-old bridges were removed by the New York City Department of Bridges in 2004 due to deterioration. Today only the underpass connects the divided cemetery property. (Courtesy of Cypress Hills Cemetery Archives.)

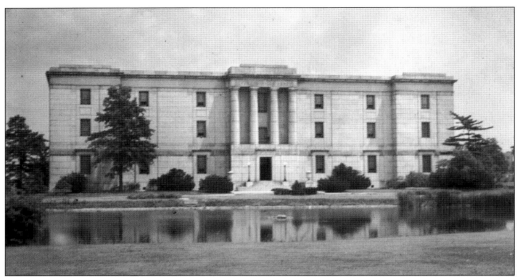

Constructed in 1929 by the New York Mausoleum Association, Inc., this classical four-level structure is called the Cypress Hills Abbey. Constructed of granite, this early photograph depicts the abbey situated on Crescent Lake. Inside, the white marble corridors are lined with thousands of crypts bearing names from the past. One of the most beautiful features of the abbey is the chapel, which was constructed of imported travertine. It is graced with beautiful stained-glass windows with spiritual themes. The windows throughout the abbey are said to have been executed by Tiffany Studios. Notables entombed here include Mae West, Jim Corbett, and Victor Moore. (Above, courtesy of Cypress Hills Cemetery Archives; below, authors' collection.)

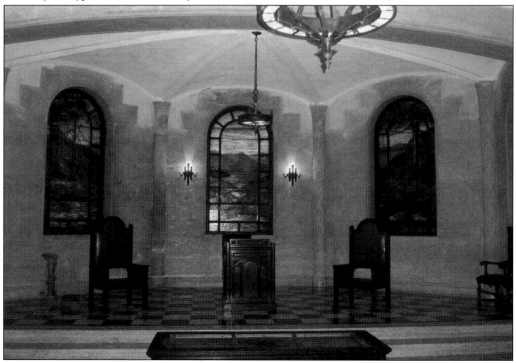

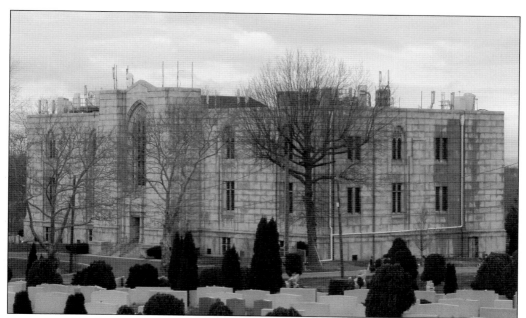

Constructed by the same company who constructed the Cypress Hills Abbey, the Memorial Abbey opened in 1931. Both abbeys had a combined construction cost of $4 million. Neo-Gothic in design, the abbey was believed to be the largest memorial structure in the world at the time. The interior has matching marble walls; family rooms; marble benches; ornate iron gates; and long, straight, seemingly endless corridors. The front of the Memorial Abbey is adorned with one of the largest stained-glass windows on Long Island. This two-story window depicts key figures from Long Island history. When opened, Cypress Hills earned the distinction of being the only cemetery in the world with two abbeys. (Both authors' collection.)

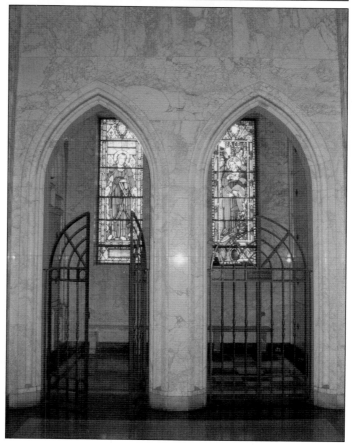

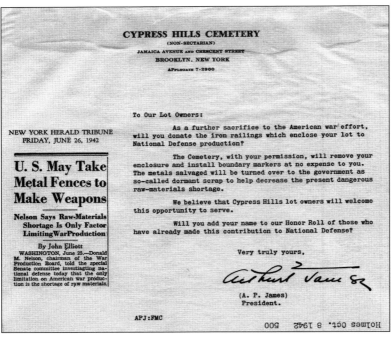

This 1942 document is a letter from the president of Cypress Hills asking permission from plot owners to remove the iron railing enclosures from their grave sites. The iron railings in turn would be donated as raw material to make various weapons and armament for the war effort. (Courtesy of Cypress Hills Cemetery Archives.)

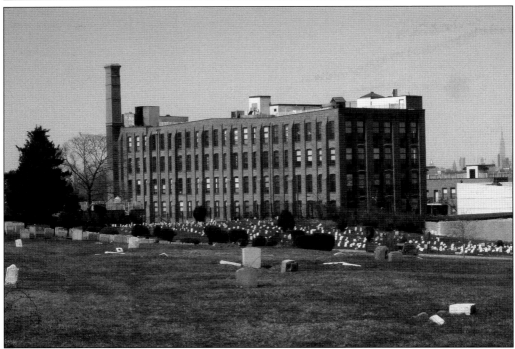

Situated on the northern edge of the cemetery grounds off Cooper Avenue was the former Barthels Manufacturing Company. Built in the early 1900s, the company provided hundreds of jobs to the Glendale community. Located in a four-story, all-brick structure, the company manufactured exquisite hair braids and all kinds of shoelaces. In 2005, the building was converted into luxury condominiums. The Empire State Building is seen in the distance at far right.

Pieter Claes Wyckoff (the first Wyckoff to leave the old country) left Holland on the good ship *Rensselaerwyck* and landed on Manhattan Island on March 4, 1636. The Wyckoff family eventually settled in Kings County and through time had a major impact on the growth and development of both Kings and Queens Counties. There are many members of the Wyckoff family buried in the Wyckoff family plot and throughout Cypress Hills Cemetery. Among them was Nicholas Wyckoff (1799–1883), who held the title of vice president of the Cypress Hills Cemetery and later served on the water commission that established the Ridgewood Reservoir. In 1938, the Wyckoffs held a family reunion. The family now numbers some 5,000 members. (Right, courtesy of Queens Public Library; below, authors' collection.)

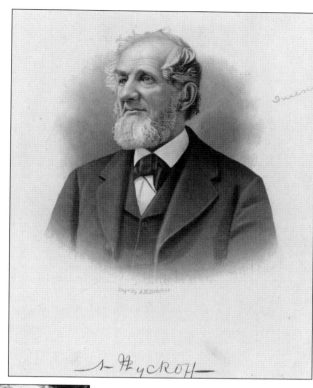

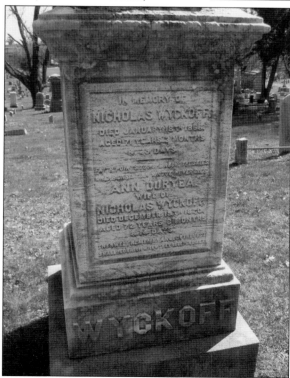

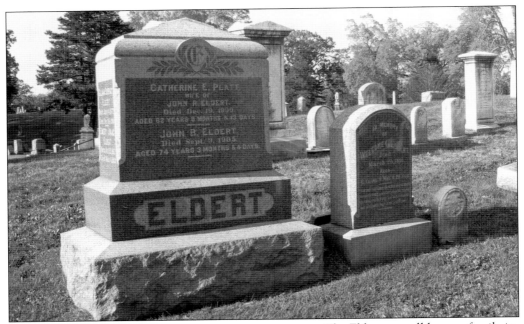

The Elderts, a well-known family in this area, owned a large farmhouse situated on Elderts Lane and Atlantic Avenue in Cypress Hills. The Elderts married into other prominent Brooklyn families; they are all in repose on the same hillside in Cypress Hills Cemetery. Before being buried in Cypress Hills, the earlier Eldert family burial plot was located in the Wyckoff-Snediker private family cemetery in Woodhaven, Queens.

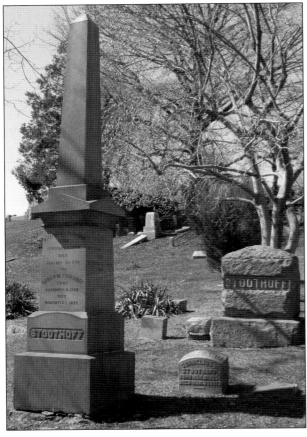

The Stoothoff family was one of the early Dutch families that came to New York in the 16th century and made a settlement in the flatlands of Brooklyn. William Stoothoff was born on February 8, 1793, and became a farmer and carpenter by trade. He died at the age of 86 in 1880. His wife, Sarah Ann, survived him by seven years; she died in 1887.

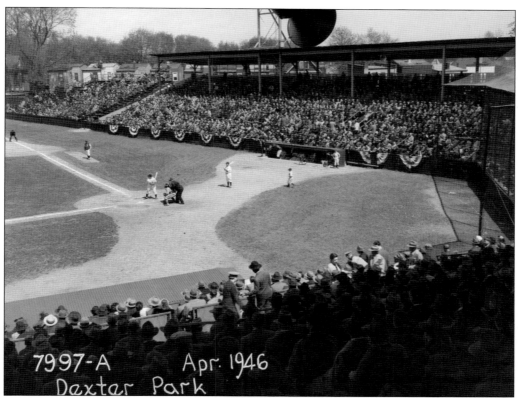

7997-A   Apr. 1946
Dexter Park

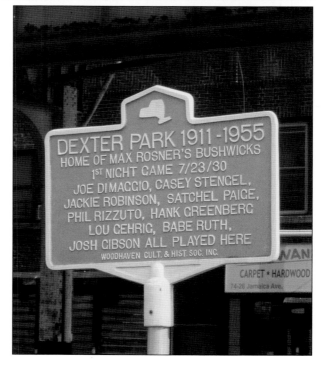

Originally home to the Brooklyn Royal Giants (part of the Negro League during the 1920s and 1930s), Dexter Park, owned by the colorful Max Rosner, later became home to the Brooklyn Bushwicks. Many semipro teams played here, producing some of the best players in baseball. Those fans who did not want to pay the small admission charge would sneak into Cypress Hills Cemetery. Once inside, they would sit on mausoleum roofs to watch the game. After the 1940s, with the arrival of television, Dexter Park slowly declined. After an initial attempt as a stock car venue, Dexter Park was razed in 1955, and the land was developed with two-family attached brick homes. In the 1990s, the Woodhaven Cultural and Historical Society erected a marker to commemorate Dexter Park. (Courtesy of Queens Public Library.)

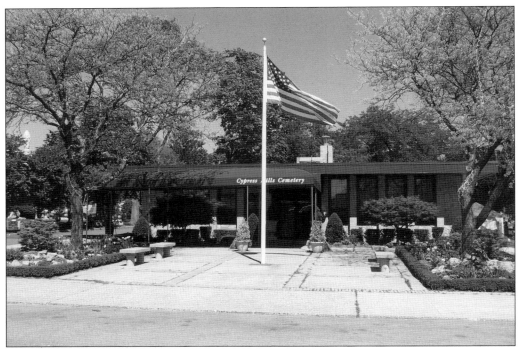

Over time Cypress Hills has had at least three different administration buildings. This one, built in 1965, is a one-story structure with an entrance plaza adorned with gardens and stone benches. The flag with a bronze plaque at the bottom was placed in recognition of the valiant sacrifices of all U.S. war veterans. (Courtesy of Cypress Hills Cemetery Archives.)

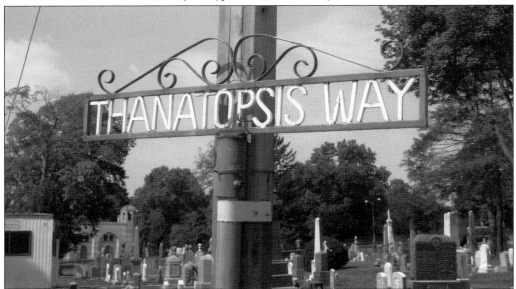

Upon entering this "city of the silent," the first roadway is appropriately named Thanatopsis Way. "Thanatopsis" is a thought-provoking poem about death, written in 1821 by William Cullen Bryant, that stirs the reader's emotions. The title is derived from the Greek word *thanatos*, meaning "death," and the suffix *opsis*, meaning "sight."

Two

MAGNIFICENT MAN-MADE MONUMENTS

The Marx stone has a perfect balance of carved serpentine stone combined with evergreens and ivy. The pure symmetry of the plot is visually appealing; two small evergreen shrubs flank the stone, while two larger shrubs create a natural backdrop. The ivy accents that grow up and around the tablet create a natural picture frame effect. Placing small loose stones on top of grave stones is a common ritual in the Jewish faith.

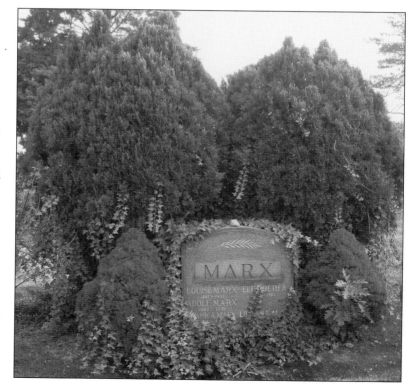

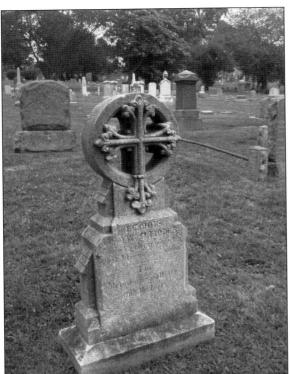

The Celtic cross is a very popular and powerful holy symbol. This beautifully sculptured two-sided stone Celtic cross is cradled upon an architectural-inspired headstone. Dating back to the fourth century, the Celtic cross is a symbol of eternity that emphasizes the endlessness of God's love as shown through Christ's sacrifice on the cross. Among ancient beliefs, the circle represents the moon, sun, or even a halo emanating from Christ.

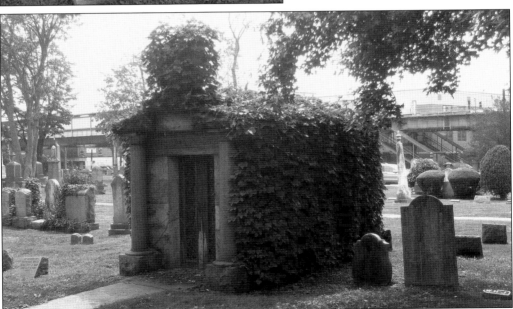

This ivy-covered mini-mausoleum is the eternal resting place for Ophelia Y. Ferguson, who died in 1886. Made of polished stone, the 8-foot-high Doric columns grace the front of this Romanesque Revival–style tomb, while the large, full ivy leaves overtake the 2-foot-tall cross that sits on the peak of the pediment. Inside are two crypts positioned on the left, a small chandelier, and a perfectly intact stained-glass window that includes an image of young Ophelia.

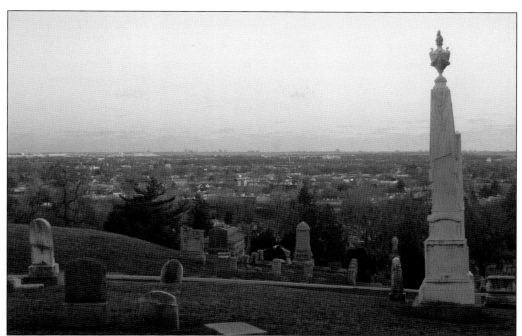

Cypress Hills Cemetery offers visitors splendid views, even as far as Jamaica Bay and the Atlantic Ocean beyond. These views, some from as high as 400 feet above sea level, create an elevated, close-to-heaven atmosphere, which can be comforting at a time of loss. This 25-foot, tassel-draped column is topped with an ornate urn, traditionally signifying the break in life; both were popular Victorian mourning symbols and were usually coupled together.

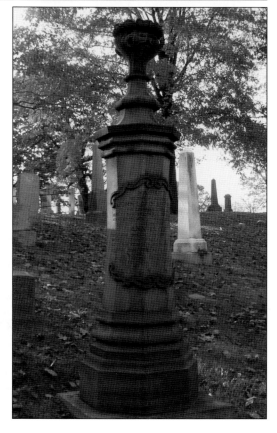

This skillfully carved 9-foot-tall brownstone grave column, resembling an oversized chess pawn, is the final resting place of the Shepperd family. This octagonal monument has a rising six-tiered base with a smooth middle section framed by an elegant scroll carving. The five-tiered top section is adorned with a large carved flower bouquet. Live flowers are as common as gravestones in cemeteries, and in each case, they have strong symbolic meaning.

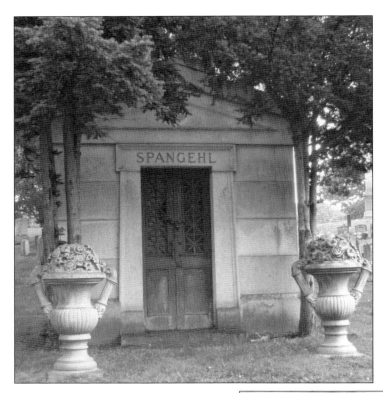

The Spangehl plot is a pleasant mixture of sculptured stone and natural elements. Small cypress trees frame the defined edges of the 10-foot-wide-by-12-foot-deep mausoleum. White marble Victorian vases measuring 4.5 feet high decorate the front on either side of the doorway. The fluted vases are topped with large sculptured flowers, adding a soft touch to the entrance. This permanent house of stone was designed and built by the Benisch brothers of Brooklyn.

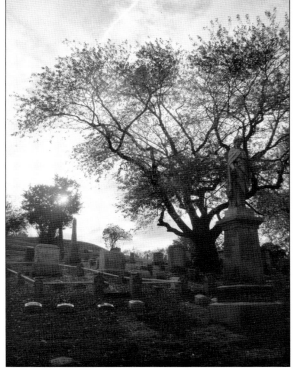

Rolling hills; tall shade trees; cloudy, sun-streaked skies; and modest grave memorials of people from our distant past are all key elements to the Cypress Hills experience. Oak trees in cemeteries stand for life everlasting and can symbolize power, authority, and victory. The Tevas statue, close to being overlooked, stands guard before the silhouetted oak and stone monuments.

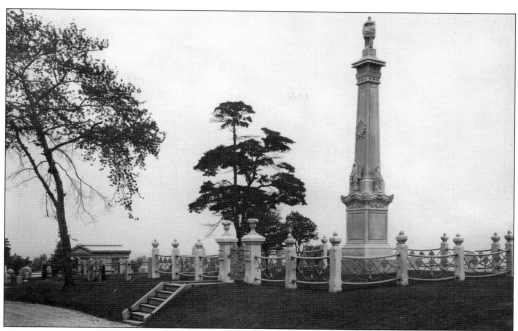

Almost unrecognizable, these two photographs were taken close to 70 years apart. Long gone are the steps, the ornate stone bollards, and the iron railings. Take note of the decorative chain work between the railings adorned with metal medallions and small tassels. In the more current photograph, a small statue stands to the right of the monument, which at one time adorned the side of the 35-foot-high white marble column. The rounded tablature stones that are placed inside the Chilson plot have since eroded to half their original size.

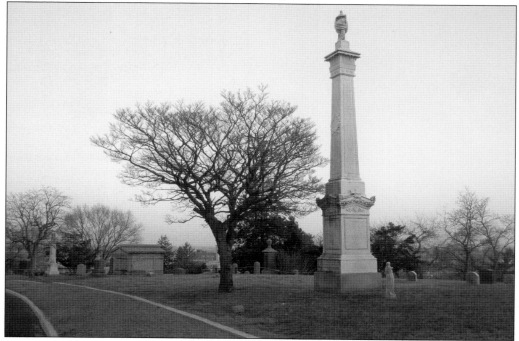

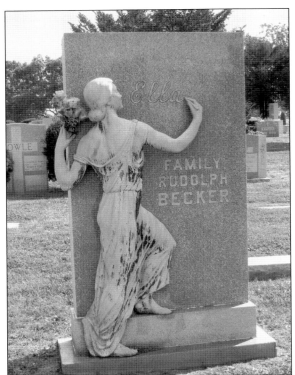

This simple die-on-base headstone is a memorial to the Rudolph Becker family. The most striking feature of the monument is the 5.5-foot-tall metal statue of a young woman writing the name "Ella" onto the smooth granite surface. Legend claims this statue is the daughter of Ella sadly immortalizing her mother's name. Notice the way the dress strap gently falls off her left shoulder as she reaches up to write.

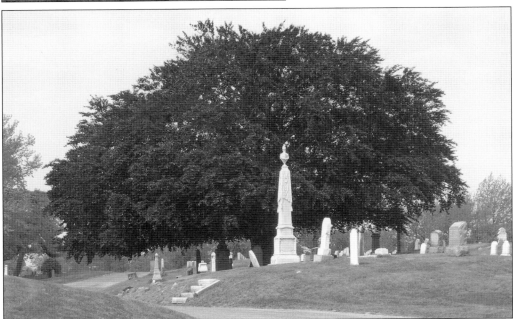

Out of all the splendid trees that give Cypress Hill its character and beauty, this beech tree is exceptionally pleasing to the eye. Perched high on the hill along William Miles Way, the tree spans over 70 feet wide. Many cemetery visitors have taken liberty in carving their initials onto its massive trunk.

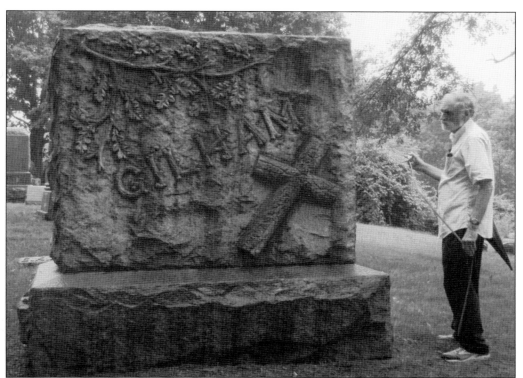

Author and local historian Allan Smith is shown here measuring this two-tier monument, which is 7 feet tall and 4.5 feet thick. Made of rock-solid, rough Quincy grey granite, it was placed here in 1918, and it is here to stay for eternity. Note the oak leaves and acorns that decorate the top of this stone monument.

For a brief time, from 1874 to 1914, an alternative to the expensive stone monument was a sand-cast zinc monument. Marketed as white bronze, this elegant name sounded special and progressive. The monument manufacturers copied the same styles and shapes as stone, but the zinc monuments were less costly. Only manufactured by the Monumental Bronze Company of Bridgeport, Connecticut, this 128-year-old zinc marker towers 25 feet into the air, making it the oldest and tallest in the cemetery.

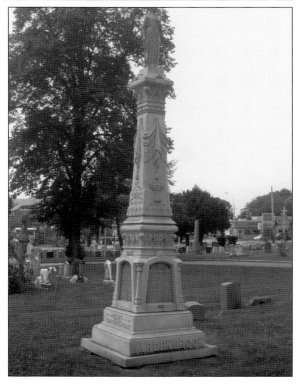

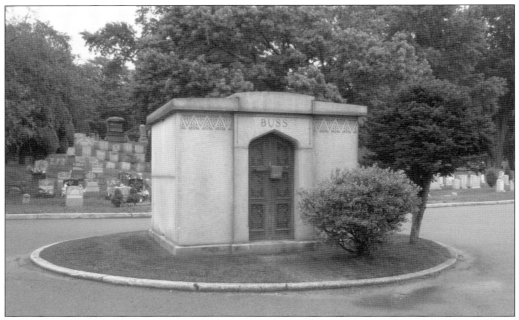

This simple, yet elegant 8.5-foot-tall square mausoleum quietly sits on its own oval grass island. Built in 1932, the structure blends together art deco and Gothic styles. The geometric band across the top reflects the art deco style, while the door frame has a pointed Gothic-shaped head pointing to the heavens. In front, a small cypress tree and shrub add balance and aesthetic beauty to the plot.

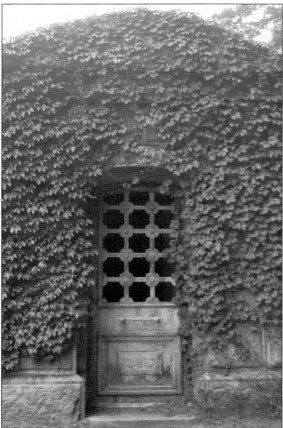

The silent darkness inside the G. W. Bloomfield mausoleum is in considerable contrast to the lush thriving ivy that grows over and around the tomb. The strong wrought-iron door is framed by hardy evergreen leaves, which denote immortality and rebirth or regeneration. Ivy covering a burial plot is said to represent friendship and fidelity. Ivy is also universally known for its ability to survive in harsh conditions and its difficult removal process.

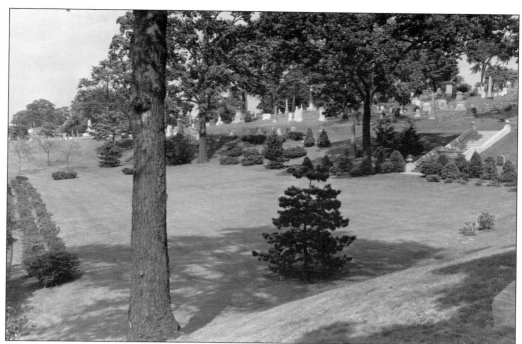

Situated in a bowl-shaped terrain, the Urn Garden is a quiet and tranquil setting of repose for the cremated remains of loved ones. Void of crowded headstones, this garden is entered via a large ascending stone staircase built into the hillside. A perfect balance of sun and shade, with well-placed landscaping and a manicured lawn, the Urn Garden offers flat, inground grave markers that emphasize the appearance of a park rather than that of a cemetery.

The cradle grave is an uncommon, yet elegant way to remember a loved one. This plot is lined with custom-cut stone edging, so that flowers can be planted inside. Cradle graves began to appear in the mid-19th century during the Victorian era (the Great Age of Death). The cradle and grave are symbols of birth followed by death, imitating the cycles of life.

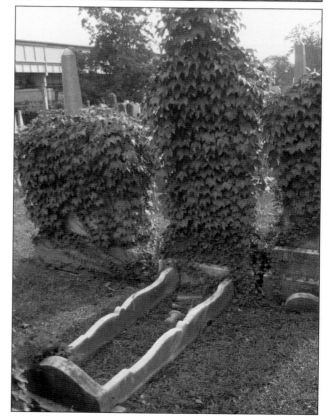

45

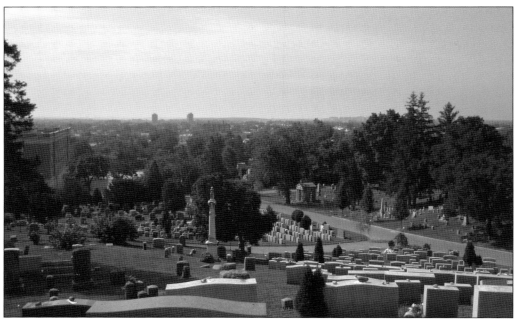

There is no cemetery in New York City that provides such a variety of breathtaking views and heavenly vantage points as Cypress Hills. The Mount of Victory plot, William Miles Way, and Lookout Point all provide wide panoramic views facing south and east. The side of Francis K. Lane High School can be seen at far left in this photograph.

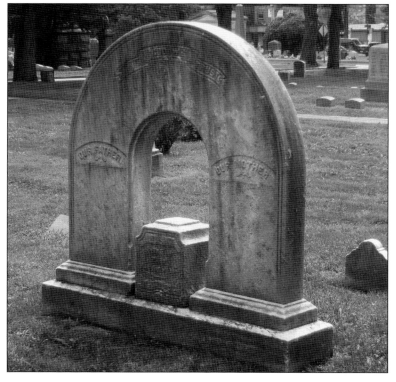

Situated in one of the oldest sections of the cemetery is the Keen family monument. This tribute to mother and father appears to be two headstones fused together creating a rainbow shape. The rainbow is one of humankind's oldest symbols of hope and eternal life. In Christian faith, the rainbow is a sign of the covenant. An arched headstone means victory over death.

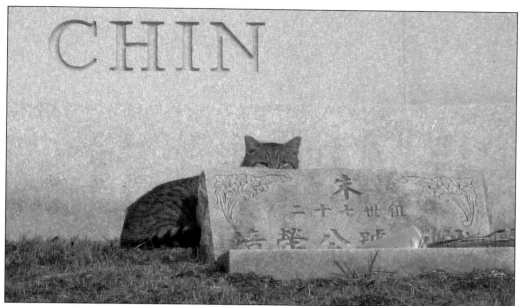

Cemeteries, although serious and associated with sadness, can be places of unexpected charm and, at times, can bring a gentle smile to one's face. Here one of God's simple creatures knows not where he is and cautiously peers over a footstone ready to make a fast break if necessary. Considering that the Chinese, by tradition, leave food at the grave for a passed loved one, this courageous cat makes its rounds. (Courtesy of Anthony Desmond.)

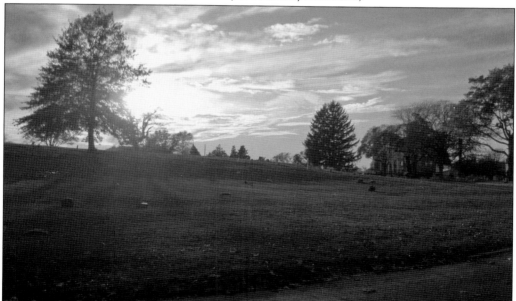

Tucked away in a northern section of Cypress Hills lies beautiful Restlawn. A few small headstones dot the gently rising landscape as a large wide-open sunset upstages them. This type of setting is visually dramatic and easily allows the visitor to connect with the elements of nature that bring forth calmness and essential healing. At the bottom, the edge of Levy Way resembles a dirt road running alongside a rolling rural field.

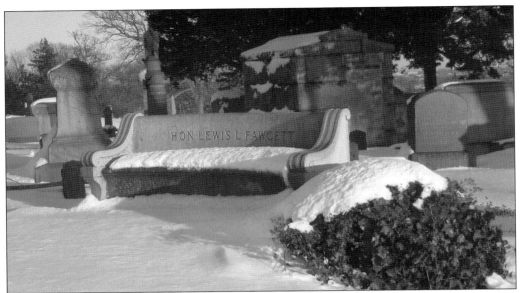

Park benches are a welcoming sight to the weary park visitor. The Fawcett burial plot invites visitors to sit down and contemplate their own mortality while taking in the quiet bucolic setting of Cypress Hills. In history, rural cemeteries were predecessors to urban parks, so it is very fitting to place this style of grave marker. This unique grave memorial is made of fine Indiana limestone that sits on a 5-inch slab of Quincy granite. There are only two bench stones like this one in the entire cemetery, and they are just feet apart from each other.

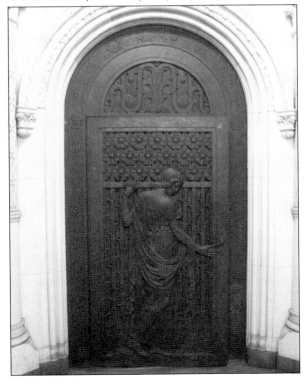

This detailed bronze relief door is located in the east wing of the Cypress Hills Abbey. Executed in the art deco style, the young woman gazes downward in a sad and solemn pose. The image takes on a ghostly quality, which is fitting considering it is in a mausoleum.

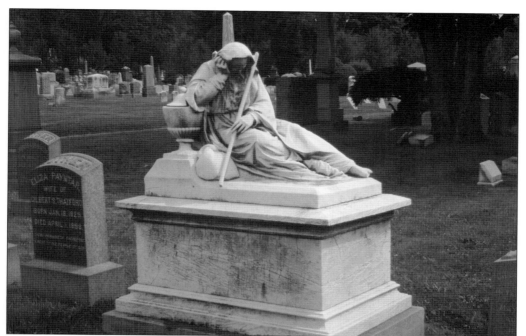

Artistically poised on top of the monument, a life-size stone figure representative of a holy shepherd has momentarily fallen into a state of slumber. Some of the earliest depictions of Christ show him as the good shepherd. As a shepherd guards his flock, this shepherd protects the resting remains of the Thatford family.

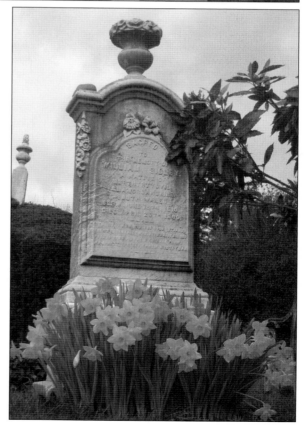

This beautiful white sandstone monument has endured the test of time, considering it is 130 years old. Unfortunately, due to weathering, the poem at the bottom is nearly illegible. However, the wording "William Sibley from South Wales who died in 1880" is still preserved. The bright, blooming yellow daffodils scent the fresh early spring air.

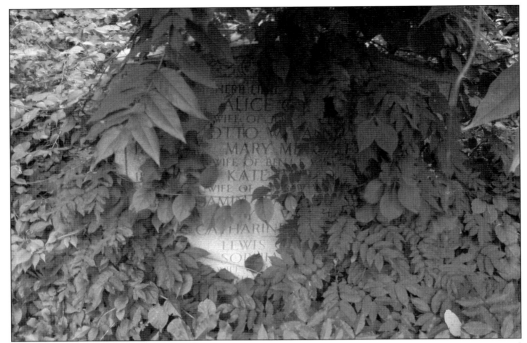

It will only be a matter of time before this headstone is lost to aggressive ivy, wild ferns, and hardy surface brush. The interpretation of plants as the embodiment of the deceased is found frequently in literature and art. From our reposing remains, the grass, the trees, the flowers, and the shrubs draw up our essence.

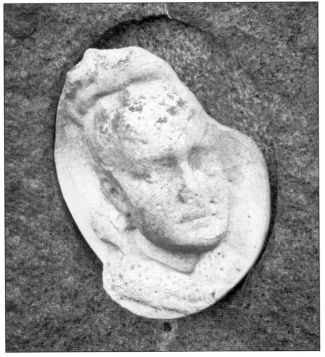

Nature can enhance man-made art, but it can also slowly destroy it. This white marble medallion containing the weathered face of a 19th-century New York resident has deteriorated over time due to the negative effects on marble from acidic rain.

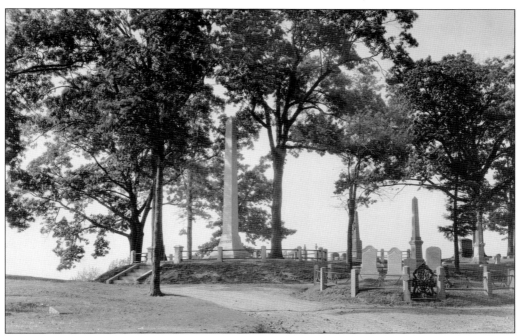

Located right on the Kings and Queens County line is the impressive 1936 Peter burial plot (seen above and below), an obelisk constructed of milky-white Indiana limestone that towers 40 feet. Stone bollards and metal railings remain, framing the monument. Unfortunately, due to harsh weather, age, and possible reckless driving, the Smith island plot (bottom right of images) has not been able to retain its ornate circular border. Even the beautiful cast-iron entrance gate has been lost. Gravel roads have been replaced with smooth paved ones, while the tall shade trees have been lost over time to an open, cloud-filled sky.

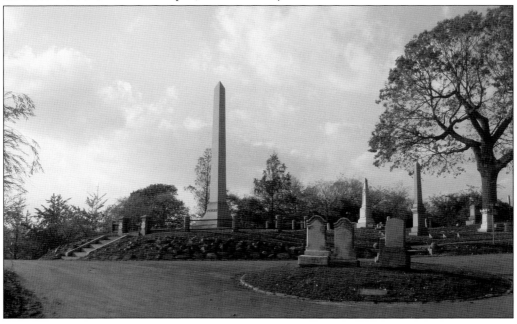

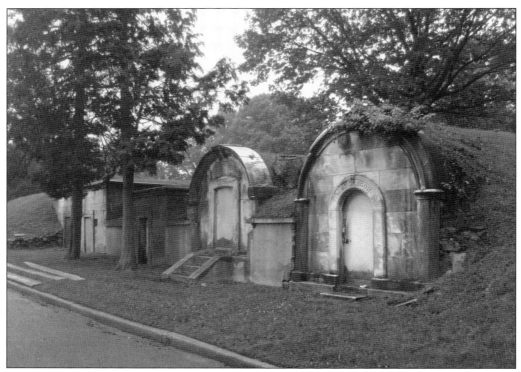

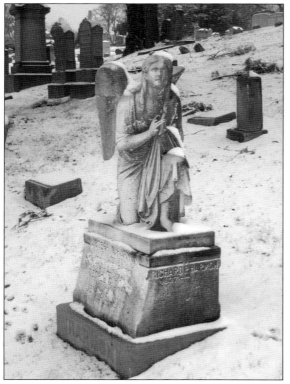

These arched hillside vaults, which naturally blend into the embankment of Cypress Hills, were built originally for display and later made available to potential buyers for purchase. A vault of this size in the 1800s would cost hundreds of dollars, while today it would cost tens of thousands of dollars. Most were built from red brick and mortar, while the arched facade is of custom-cut white marble. These vaults were built to accommodate at least 15 deceased, making them attractive to large extended families.

Angels play a vital spiritual role here on earth, as they do in the heavens. They guard the tombs of the deceased and guide the souls of the departed to the heavens. Angels will actively pray for the souls in purgatory and remind the living visitors to think heavenward. Here the natural element of freshly fallen snow enhances the beauty of this kneeling angel monument.

Three

MYSTERIOUS MARKINGS AND SECRET SYMBOLS

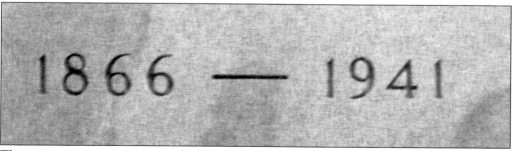

The most common, yet most overlooked marking on a headstone is the dash that separates the year of birth from the year of death. The dash, though small in size, has great significance in that it encapsulates the life that was lived. It represents life's summation and how that individual will be remembered in the future. The dash is also an important reminder for the living to pause and reflect upon one's own mortality.

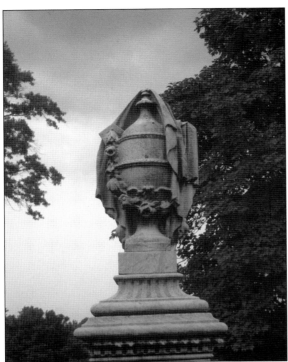

The shroud-draped urn is a very popular symbol in cemeteries. Cremated ashes would be placed in an urn, which is derived from the Latin word *uro*, meaning "to burn." As inground burials became more popular, the urn still continued to be an object closely associated with death. Christians used the funeral urn to represent the discarded body and added the shroud or "veil of death" to symbolize that the soul has departed the body to eternally rest with God in heaven.

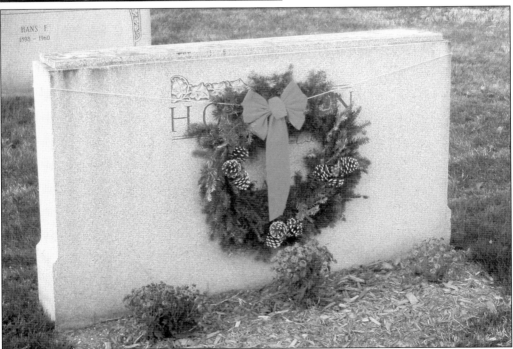

Normally placed during the holiday season, this popular grave decoration has powerful symbolism. The open wreath, pictured here, implies the victory of a good life—an idea originating in the neoclassical period when Romans would crown soldiers with laurel wreaths for extreme feats of bravery.

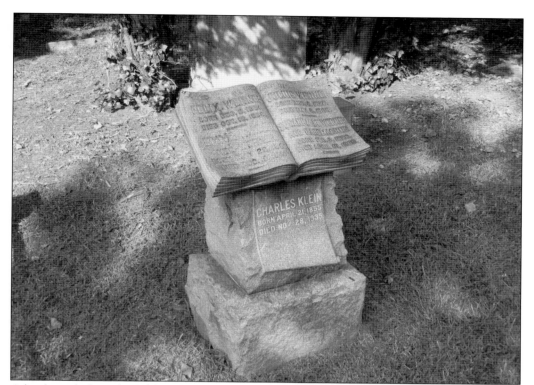

A book symbolizes the Bible or how one's life story is portrayed. The open book (above) can be compared to a person with an open heart or a person that freely expressed his or her thoughts and feelings to the world and God. A closed book (right) can signify that one's life has been lived and completed and that the story has been told or ended. A book on a gravestone can also more literally depict someone who enjoyed learning; a scholar; or someone who worked as a writer, bookseller, or publisher. It can even represent a favorite prayer, memory, or book of the deceased as well. The two-tiered stone monument above with an open book memorializes Charles Klein.

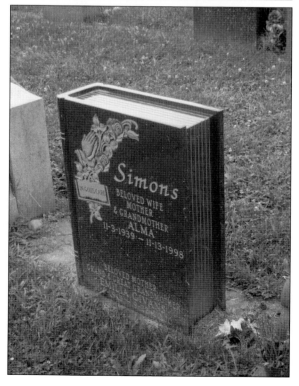

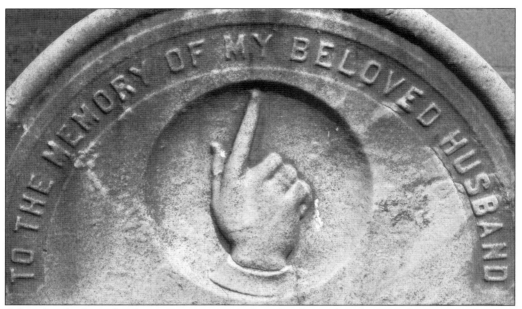

A hand with the index finger pointing upward implies hope that the spirit has risen to heaven, while a hand with a forefinger pointing down implies God reaching down for the soul. The hand is an important symbol of life; hands carved into gravestones represent the deceased's relationship with other human beings and with God. Cemetery hand carvings tend to be shown doing one of four things: blessing, clasping, pointing, or praying.

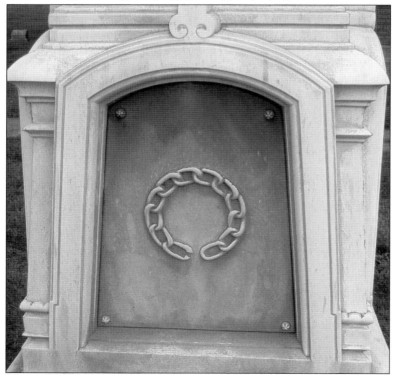

A series of chain links in a complete circle can symbolize the circle of life, and each link can represent a family member. Medieval thinkers believed that a golden chain bound the soul to the body. A broken link on a headstone suggests the severance and subsequent release of the spirit from the body. A broken link can also be simply interpreted as a life lost.

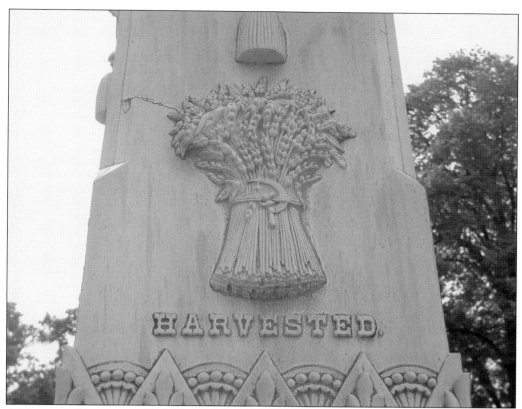

A Victorian Christian symbol, harvested wheat signifies the divine harvest at the end of life or a fulfilled life. It can also symbolize the body of Christ.

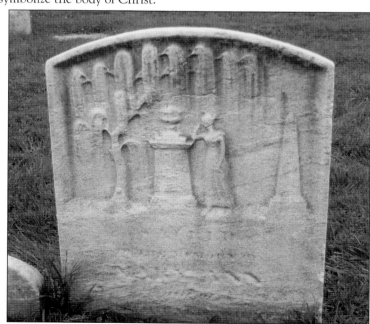

Carved into this simple, flat headstone is a mourning figure visiting the final resting place of a dearly departed. On the tablet to the left is a weeping willow tree, which signifies sadness, grief, and perpetual mourning. There are many weeping willow trees that grace the Cypress Hills Cemetery grounds.

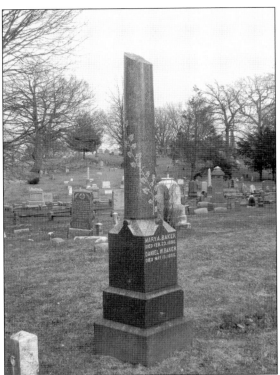

A broken column can be confusing to a cemetery visitor. One would think it was broken due to damage, age, or even vandalism. Many columns are intentionally carved in the broken form to indicate someone who died young or in the prime of their life. Another theory relates to ancient Greek and Roman civilizations. Since the men and women who built monuments such as the Parthenon are now long dead, this broken column image represents the eventual ruin or decomposition of us all.

Seen in both Christian and Jewish cemeteries, doves or birds imply resurrection, innocence, and peace. A dove descending, as pictured here, represents a descent from heaven, assurance of a safe passage. An ascending dove represents the transport of the departed's soul to heaven. A dove lying dead stands for a life cut short. A dove holding an olive branch signifies that the soul has reached divine peace in heaven.

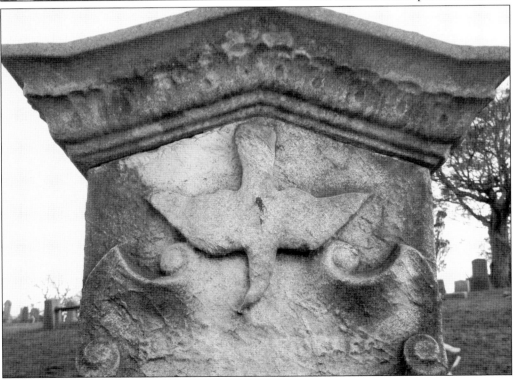

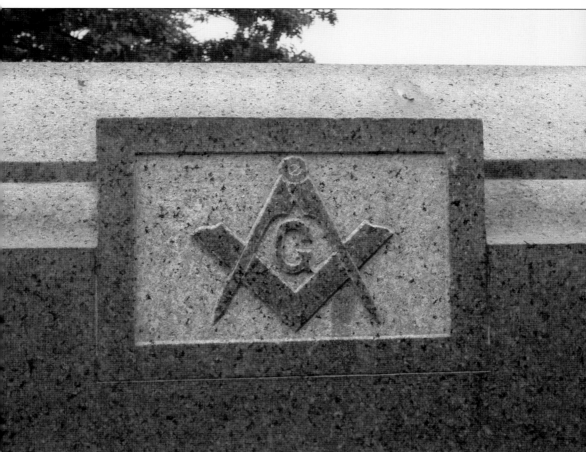

Under the fatherhood of a supreme being, Freemasonry is the oldest and largest worldwide fraternity dedicated to the Brotherhood of Man. The most common symbol of the Free and Accepted Masons is the compass and square, standing respectively for faith and reason. The compass is used by builders to draw circles and lay off measurements along a line. Masons use it as a symbol of self-control with the intention of drawing a proper boundary around personal desires and to remain within the lines. A builder's square in the Masonic symbol is used by carpenters and stonemasons to measure perfect right angles. In Masonry, this signifies the ability to use teachings of conscience and mortality to measure and verify the rightness of one's action. The letter G, usually found in the center of the square and compass, is said to stand for "Geometry" or "God." George Washington and Benjamin Franklin were both proud members of this fraternal order.

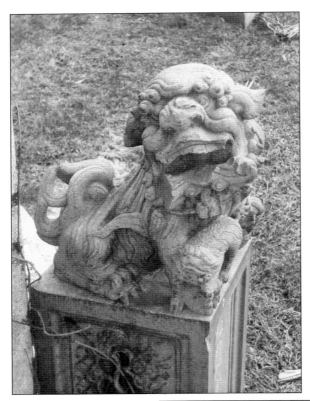

The foo dog of Asia has been called the "Lion of Buddha," and that name is very accurate, since it is a lion and not a dog at all. In Asian culture, foo dogs are believed to have protective powers and are normally placed at entrances to guard and protect. Here a female foo dog stands guard at a Chinese burial plot. The female foo holds down a kitten, which signifies her ruling of the domestic life, the raising of children, and the overall management of the household.

An anchor was regarded in ancient times as a symbol of safety and was adopted by Christians to signify hope and steadfastness. The anchor can also indicate the anchoring influence of Christ. Some historians strongly believe the anchor, during certain times, was used as a disguised cross. The anchor can be a sign to honor seamanship and may mark the grave of a seaman or as a tribute to St. Nicholas, patron saint of seamen. An anchor with a broken chain signifies the cessation of life.

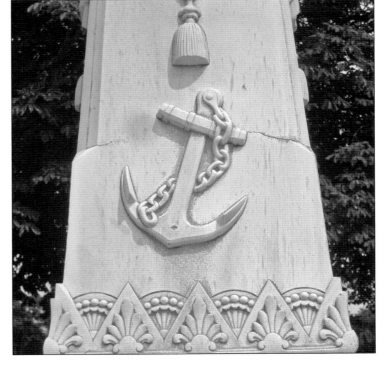

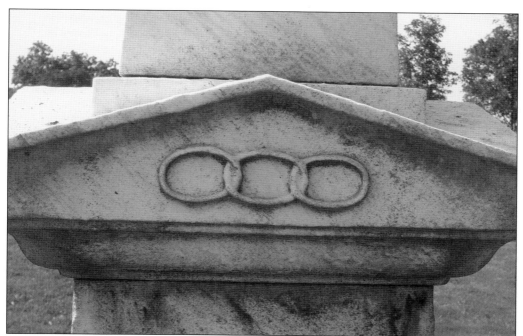

The simple, yet poignant marking of three joined circles is the internationally recognized symbol of the Independent Order of Odd Fellows (IOOF), a fraternal organization also known as "The Three Links Fraternity." The three links stand for friendship, love, and faith. The organization focused on charitable works. In 17th-century England, it was "odd" to find people pursuing projects for the benefit of all humankind—hence the name.

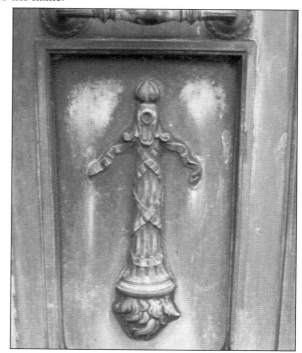

The inverted torch appears odd or even disturbing, but in funerary art, it is a true cemetery symbol. It signifies life in the next realm or a life extinguished. It directly communicates death or the passing of the soul into the next life. An upright lit torch represents everlasting life and immortality.

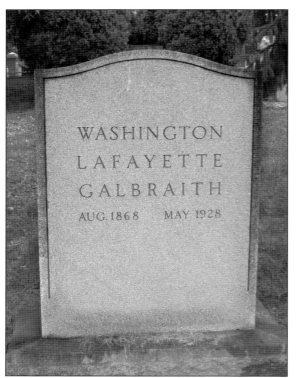

Outside of an intriguing name on a headstone, a common shape for tablature headstones in cemeteries across America is the serpentine or curved top. A headstone is like a pillar that stands erect, meant to be read like a book. Above all else, no matter how immovable this stone might be, a serpentine top indicates the determination of the human creative forces needed to cut hard stone. The sweep of the serpentine is a symbol of the freedom of the spiritual being that can now move in any fashion desired, unrestricted by human forces.

WASHINGTON
LAFAYETTE
GALBRAITH

AUG. 1868   MAY 1928

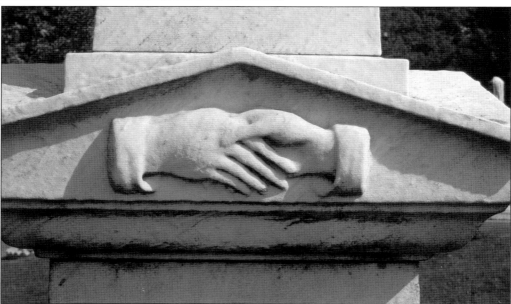

The hand may be the most distinctly human appendage, as hands are essential to accomplishing many aspects of daily life like reaching, touching, holding, scratching, and doing much of the work required to exist in society. From that fact of life, the hand also points to spiritual matters, especially in cemeteries. Clasping, holding, or shaking hands symbolizes matrimony or other close human relationships.

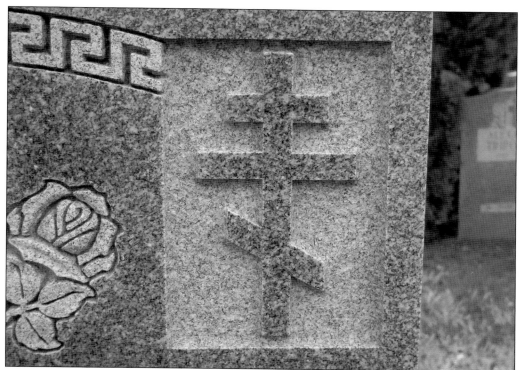

The Byzantine cross is often used by Eastern European Catholics or the Russian Orthodox. The footrest positioned at a slant represents a footrest wrenched loose from Christ writhing in intense physical suffering. The lower side symbolizes hell, the fate of sinners, while the elevated side symbolizes heaven.

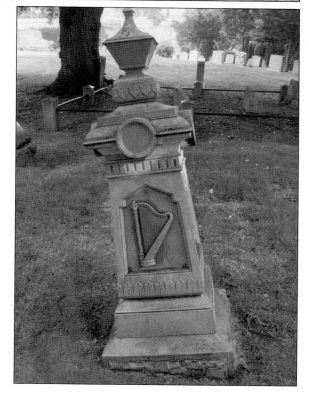

This four-sided zinc monument leaning slightly has a musical instrument clearly placed on one side. An angelic symbol, the harp glorifies and praises God in the heavens with soothing distinct musical string tones that only a harp can produce. A popular feature in the Victorian period, this monument is 128 years old. Sometimes, a broken string would be included representing the breaking away of mortal life.

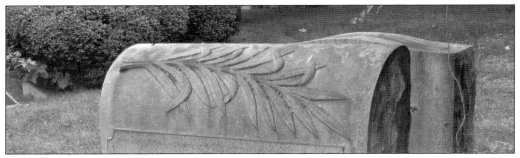

Early Christians used palm branches to symbolize the victory of the faithful over enemies of the soul. In Christian art, the martyrs were shown holding palms representing the victory of spirit over flesh. In Judaism, palm leaves signify peace and plenty and are one of the four species used in daily prayers on the feast of Sukkot.

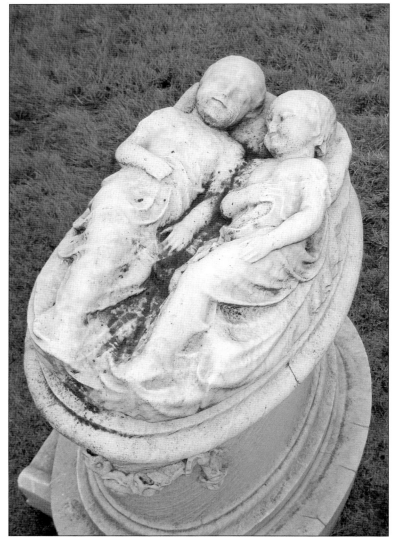

During the Victorian era (1837–1901), funerary architecture evolved to incorporate elaborate sculptures filled with symbolism and meaning. There was a high mortality rate during this period, and a sleeping child or baby signifies the premature or unexpected passing of the innocent. These small statuettes often appear with very few clothes, suggesting that during their brief lives they had nothing to hide.

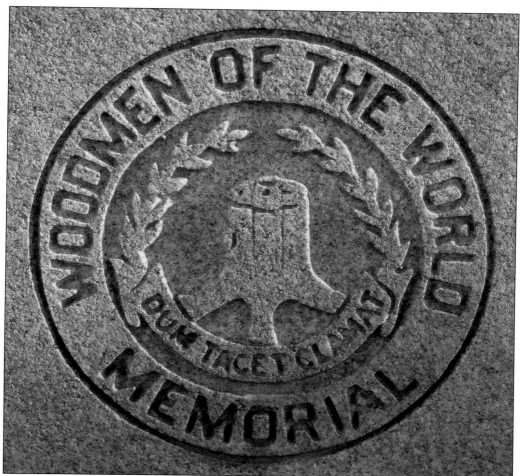

Founded by Joseph Cullen Root on June 6, 1890, Woodmen of the World (WOW) is one of the largest fraternal benefit societies. Although its focus was life insurance and death benefits to its dedicated members, the Woodmen fraternity, through its local lodges, was an active force in aiding communities in need. The Woodmen trademark, which at times can include a log, ax, or wedge, is usually carved into the front of the headstone. This WOW symbol consists of a tree stump, the strongest section of the tree, coupled with the Latin phrase *Dum Tacet Clamat*, meaning "Though Silent, He Speaks," placed underneath.

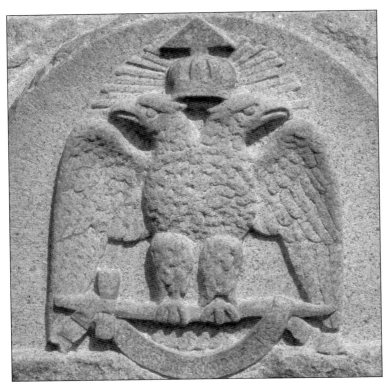

The two-headed eagle with wings outstretched while perched on a sword is recognized as one of the oldest symbols known to humankind. This emblem is that of the Scottish Rite of Freemasonery. A Prussian crown surmounts this symbol with an arrow pointing toward heaven, which celebrates the soul's achievement and the glory of life after death. At the bottom is the Latin phrase *Deus Meumque Jus*, meaning "God and my Right."

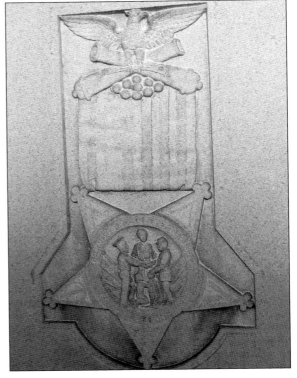

Carved directly into the face of this headstone is a striking medal that indicates the deceased was a proud member of the Grand Army of the Republic (GAR). The GAR was a fraternal organization of brave men who fought and were honorably discharged from the Union army during the Civil War. The medal incorporates a surmounted eagle over crossed cannons. The five-point star is strongly associated with the U.S. military and is based on its use in the American flag. In the relief, a Union officer is being honored while his loving family stands close by.

Similar to the Freemasonry order, the Fire Square Club of New York City was established in the mid-1800s. As firefighters, the Square Club members were active in social activities and provided community outreach to the less fortunate. There was also a Police Square Club of New York City during this time.

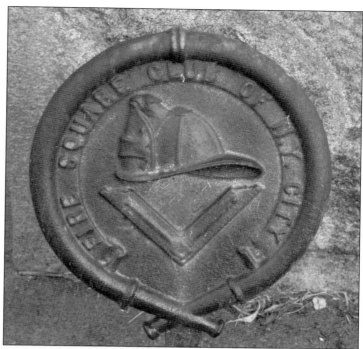

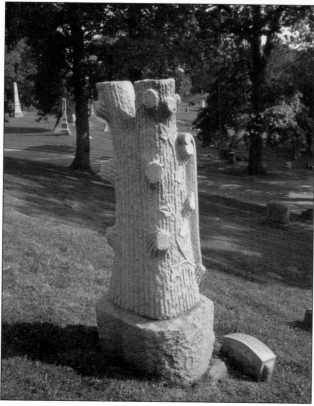

A tombstone in the shape of a tree trunk is symbolic of the brevity of life. The number of broken or sawed off branches may indicate the number of deceased family members buried at the site.

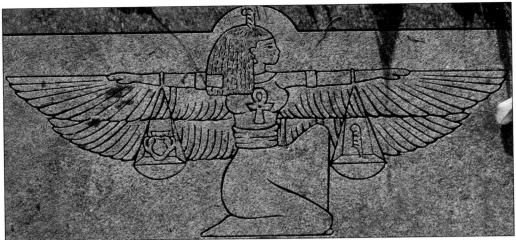

Egyptian culture is filled with fascinating theories about life, yet even more about death. Carved into a flat headstone is the mother of all Egyptian goddesses, Isis. In mythology, Isis was known as the goddess of magic, life, and rebirth. Her awesome powers included the resurrection of her dead husband by fanning her beautiful protective wings over his lifeless body. Notice the Ankh cross, taken from the Egyptian hieroglyphics image, meaning "eternal life."

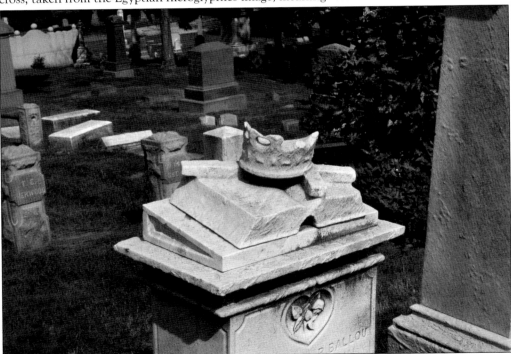

A powerful religious symbol, the cross and crown signifies both victory over death and Christianity. The only grave marker of its kind in the cemetery, the cross and crown sit on top of an open bible, another major reference to Christianity. Take notice that these three religious symbols all rest on a book prop, creating the impression of a lectern or an altar that a minister or a clergyman uses to give sermons. If the cross were placed through the crown it would indicate the deceased's membership of the York Rite Masons as well as a symbol of authority.

Four

NAMES THAT ECHO FROM THE PAST

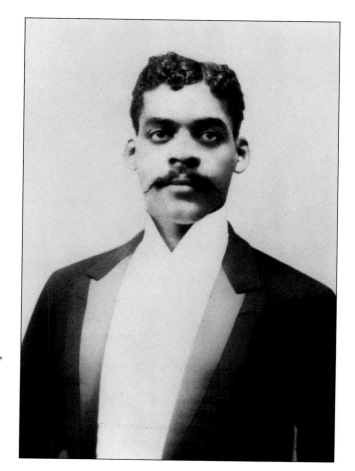

Arturo Alfonso Schomburg (1874–1938) is buried in Locust Grove. A gifted writer, cultural activist, and tireless collector, Schomburg is one of the best-known names among African American scholars. Less known is that he was actually Puerto Rican. Schomburg amassed the world's most comprehensive collection of books, manuscripts, paintings, etchings, and memorabilia directly related to the history of black culture. The Schomburg Center for Research in Black Culture in Harlem is named in his honor. (Courtesy of New York Public Library.)

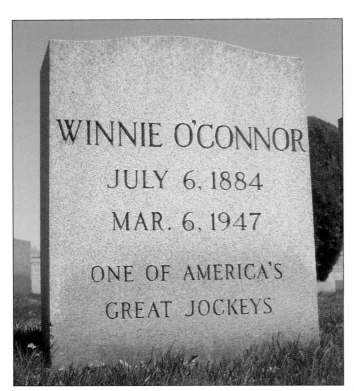

WINNIE O'CONNOR

JULY 6, 1884

MAR. 6, 1947

ONE OF AMERICA'S

GREAT JOCKEYS

Winfield O'Conner (1884–1947) learned at an early age the key strategies to becoming a successful, dynamic horse jockey. Trained by legendary horse trainer Bill Daily, O'Conner won his first race in 1896 at age 12. In 1901, he was the nation's leading rider after winning 24 percent of his races. During one race, O'Conner was paid $10,000 whether he won or lost. In 1956, nine years after O'Conner died, he was inducted into the National Museum of Racing Hall of Fame. He is interred in Laurel Green.

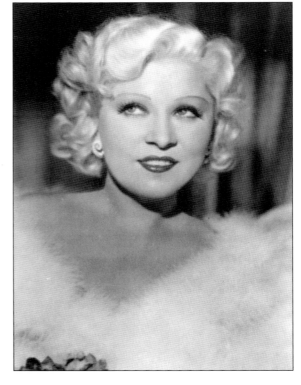

Mae West (1893–1980) is entombed in Cypress Hills Abbey. Born 15 short blocks from the cemetery, West is accredited in establishing the prototype of the Hollywood sex symbol. Her salacious eye-rolling, her suggestive strutting, and her thinly veiled innuendoes spawned a string of risqué movie comedies throughout the 1920s and 1930s. By 1936, she became the highest-paid woman in the United States, earning over $400,000 a year. Her sexually charged one-liners are legendary, especially at a time when censorship ruled the industry. (Courtesy of Cypress Hills Cemetery Archives.)

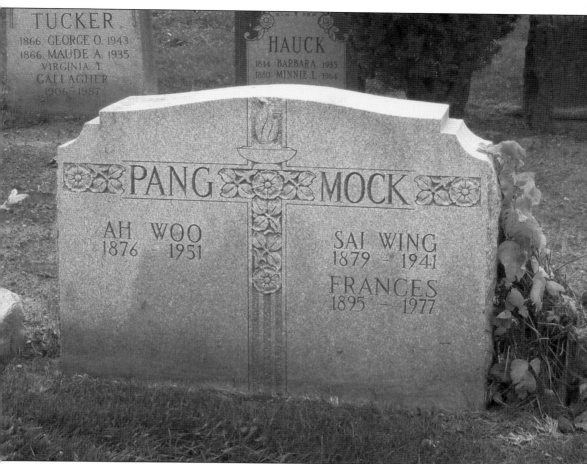

TUCKER
1866 GEORGE O. 1943
1866 MAUDE A. 1935
VIRGINIA T.
GALLAGHER
1906–1987

HAUCK
1844 BARBARA 1935
1880 MINNIE L. 1964

PANG
AH WOO
1876 – 1951

MOCK
SAI WING
1879 – 1941
FRANCES
1895 – 1977

Sai Wing Mock (1879–1941), also known as "Mock Duck," was the colorful gang leader of the Hip Sing Tong in New York's Chinatown for the first three decades of the 20th century. During this time, Tongs controlled the Chinatown opium dens and, most importantly, the gambling parlors and their proceeds. The Hip Sing Tong's most notorious rival was the On Leong Tong. Gun-blazing, hatchet-flying street wars were legendary. The phrase "hatchet man" comes from these battles because assassin's hid small axes in their long shirtsleeves. Gang leader Duck, standing at 5 feet, 3 inches, was a curious mixture of bravery and cowardice. Although a poor marksman, he earned a reputation for bravery for the utter disregard of his own life. Surprisingly, after 30 years of sporadic violence and through all the gunfire, Duck was only shot once. In 1912, he was sent to Sing Sing prison for the illegal operation of a policy game. When released in 1934, he announced to the *Brooklyn Daily Eagle* that he was through with his old life and had every intention of becoming a respectable citizen of Brooklyn. Mock died of natural causes in 1941 at the age of 62 and is buried in Greenlawn.

Ethel Cuff Black (1880–1977) is buried in Section 16. Born into a prominent African American family, Black was educated in public schools until she entered the Industrial School for Colored Youth in Bordentown, New Jersey. There she received the highest scholastic average, allowing her to enter Howard University in 1910, a prestigious college for African Americans. In 1913, Black became one of the 22 founding sisters of Delta Sigma Theta sorority, the largest African American Greek-lettered sorority in the world. (Courtesy of Delta Sigma Theta.)

Henry Phillips (1825–1911) is interred in Section 4. Living in Cranford, New Jersey, Henry Phillips the engineer became Henry Phillips the inventor. He spent many years working on a perpetual-motion machine and an early compressed-air machine, both of which eventually paid off. In 1896, he received a patent on a device that would be found in homes across America and the world; Henry invented the kitchen range hood. His brother Charles Phillips also went down in history. He invented Phillips Milk of Magnesia.

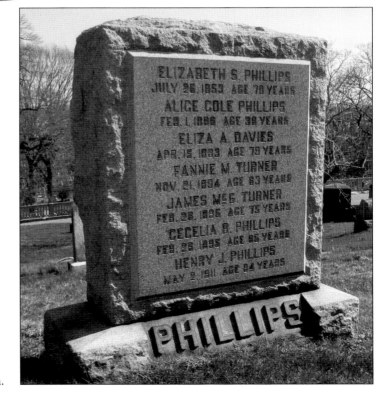

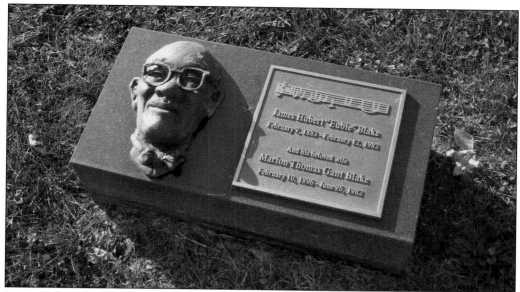

James Hubert "Eubie" Blake (1883–1983) is interred in Section 11. Blake was a composer and lyricist and excelled as a pianist of ragtime, jazz, and popular music. Eubie's extremely long fingers would hop and skip across the ivories with ease, giving him a signature style. In 1921, he wrote the musical score for *Shuffle Along*, the first Broadway musical ever produced and directed by an African American. At the age of 94, he was awarded the Presidential Medal of Freedom. In 1983, the same year Eubie died, he was inducted into the Big Band and Jazz Hall of Fame.

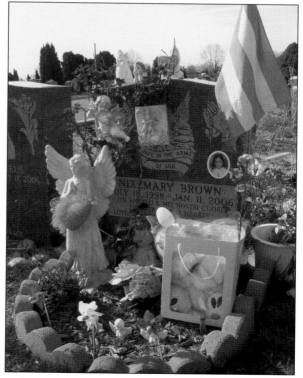

Nixmary Brown (1998–2006) was regularly abused by her biological mother and stepfather. Her stepfather, in a fit of uncontrollable rage, repeatedly slammed Nixmary's head into a bathtub. Her untimely, highly publicized, gruesome death greatly impacted New York City's Administration for Children's Services and set forth nationwide reforms in the childcare system. Nixmary's Law, instituted in 2006, is designed to deter or prevent child abuse by charging parents with first-degree murder. She is buried in Section 14.

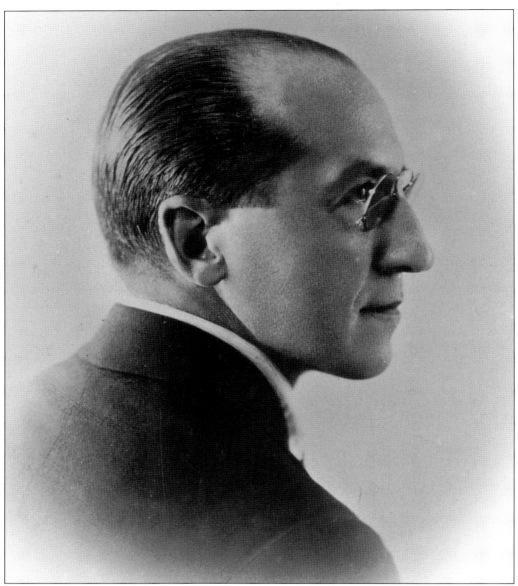

Piet Mondrian (1872–1944) is buried in Crescent Knoll. Born in the Netherlands, Mondrian was an early-20th-century artist who made significant contributions to the De Stijl ("the style") movement. Heavily influenced by the avant-garde trends such as cubism, his most celebrated style was the use of vertical and horizontal black lines forming complex rectangular shapes filled with primary colors, along with black and white. Through this approach he evolved a nonrepresentational form he coined neoplasticism. At the advent of World War II, Mondrian fled to New York City, giving him a whole new canvas of art inspiration. In 1942, his painting *Broadway Boogie-Woogie*, which today is displayed in the Museum of Modern Art, was highly influential in the school of abstract geometric painting. In 1944, working on *Victory Boogie-Woogie*, Piet died unexpectedly of pneumonia. This prominent painter has been deceased for over 65 years, yet today his artistic influence lives on in architecture, fashion, cosmetics, and even album covers. (Courtesy of Mondrian Huis Museum.)

Otto Huber Sr. (1839–1889) is buried in Section 1. Born in Baden, Germany, Huber immigrated to the United States in 1862. In 1866, Huber started brewing beer, and in 1886, he bought his first brewery, which he sold two years later. Huber then built the Otto Huber Brewery, one of the largest and most productive breweries in the East, at 242 Meserole Street near Bushwick Avenue. Huber's signature brew was Golden Rod Lager. After Huber's death in 1889, his sons continued to operate the brewery until 1920.

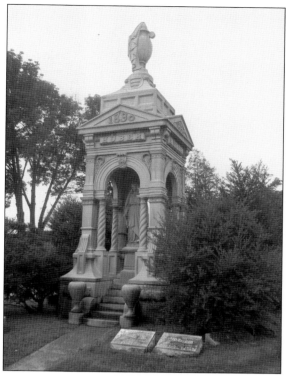

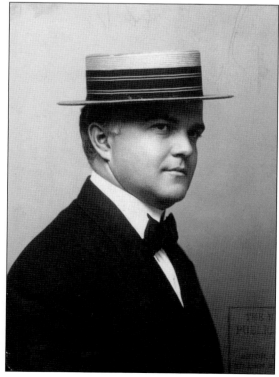

Victor Moore (1876–1962) was a versatile stage and screen actor who specialized in playing shy, bumbling, but well-meaning comical characters. Already a veteran of Broadway and vaudeville, Moore made his film debut in 1915. His best-known stage role was in the 1931 musical *Of Thee I Sing*. His long, illustrious career included 58 films and 21 Broadway plays. A heart attack took Moore's life at age 86. He is entombed in Cypress Hills Abbey. (Courtesy of New York Public Library.)

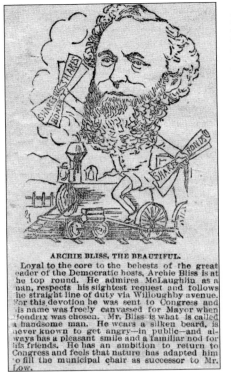

Archibald Meserole Bliss (1838–1923) held many high positions in life, including a respectable five terms as a U.S. congressman. After an unsuccessful bid for mayor of Brooklyn in 1867, Bliss became president of the Bushwick Railroad Company. Bliss was elected into the 44th Congress and was reelected three times (1875–1883). In 1885, he was elected for another two terms and stepped down in 1888. After politics, he entered the real estate field until his death at age 85. He is interred in Section 6. (Courtesy of New York Public Library.)

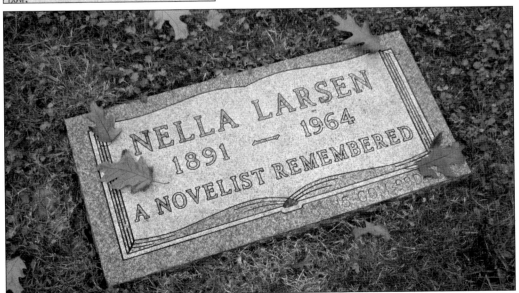

Nella Larsen (1891–1964) was a prominent African American novelist and short-story writer. During the 1920s and 1930s, Larsen directly addressed issues about her gender and race. Her two novels, *Quicksand* and *Passing*, relate to some of her own personal experiences and beliefs that depict her characters in racial and sexual confusion. Though her literary work was brief, the quality of what she wrote earned her high regard by her contemporaries and today's writing critics. She is buried in Section 15.

The Collyer brothers, Homer (1883–1947) and Langley (1886–1947), are interred in Section 5. Regarded as New York's greatest hermit hoarders, Homer and Langley, two educated but eccentric brothers, made history when their three-story Harlem brownstone was raided by police. What the police found inside went down in pack rat history. Crammed in from floor to ceiling was a long list of collected junk and useless garbage. Besides countless bundles of newspapers and books, they found several baby carriages, rusted bikes, hundreds of guns, chandeliers, three dressmaker dummies, 14 pianos, human organs pickled in jars, a horse's jawbone, numerous musical instruments, and to top it all off, a complete chassis of a Model T Ford. The police marveled at the small mazelike pathways throughout the house amidst the stacked items that ultimately led to the brother's painful demise. Langley, feeling paranoid, booby-trapped the house to ward off thieves and curiosity seekers. Unfortunately, while tending to his blind and weak younger brother, he set off one of his own traps; his body was discovered several weeks later buried under bundles of heavy, wet newspapers, piles of suitcases, and bread boxes. The police discovered Homer's lifeless body on the third floor, dead from starvation. (Courtesy of Cypress Hills Cemetery Archives.)

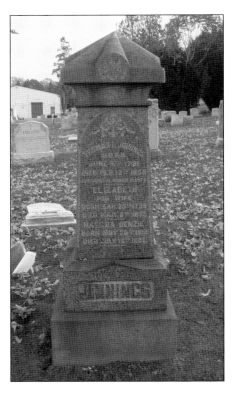

Thomas Jennings (1791–1859) is buried in Section 11. A clothier and tailor, Jennings was the first African American to receive a U.S. patent, which was for a dry cleaning method he coined "Dry Scouring." He was an outspoken advocate to end slavery in the South. Jennings was the founder of the *Freedom Journal* and one of the original founders of the oldest and largest black congregation in the United States, the Abyssinian Baptist Church in Harlem.

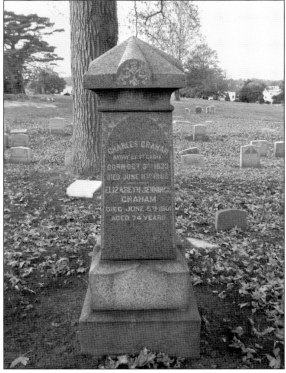

Elizabeth Jennings Graham (1830–1901) is interred in Section 11. In 1854, Elizabeth boarded a public streetcar in the Lower East Side only to be forcibly ejected by the conductor. Elizabeth's activist father, Thomas Jennings, decided to take legal action. Jennings hired the pro-abolitionist Culver-Parker law firm to represent Elizabeth against the Third Avenue Railroad Company. The law firm appointed a 23-year-old lawyer, Chester A. Arthur, who later served as the 21st president of the United States, to handle the highly publicized case. Their 1855 court victory led to the integration of New York City streetcars.

James "Gentleman Jim" Corbett (1866–1933), also nicknamed the "Father of Modern Boxing," brought class and style to boxing. He innovated fast jabs and the hook and possessed excellent footwork. Standing at 6 foot, 2 inches with a reach of 73 inches, Corbett's talents won him the heavyweight title in 1872. After winning 16 of 25 professional fights (four by knockouts), he retired in 1897. Corbett was elected posthumously into the International Boxing Hall of Fame in 1990. He is entombed in Cypress Hills Abbey. (Courtesy of Library of Congress.)

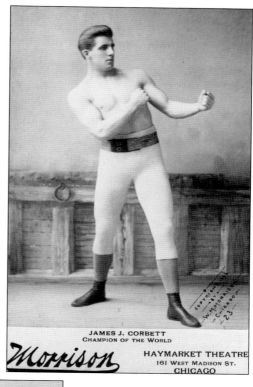

JAMES J. CORBETT
CHAMPION OF THE WORLD

Morrison

HAYMARKET THEATRE
161 WEST MADISON ST.
CHICAGO

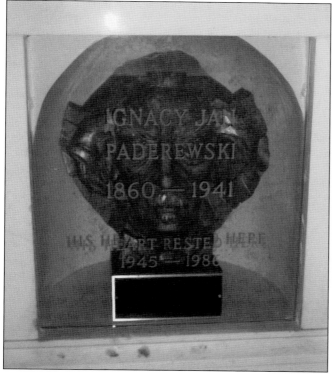

Ignacy Jan Paderewski (1860–1941) was a world-famous pianist, composer, and an outspoken Polish politician who strongly opposed both socialist and communist beliefs. His last wish was to have his heart, not his body, remain in the United States until Poland once again becomes a free country. Between the years of 1941 to 1986, Paderewski's heart was placed in a small niche in the Cypress Hills Abbey, where it remained until it was removed and placed in Our Lady of Cxestochowia Shrine in Doylestown, Pennsylvania.

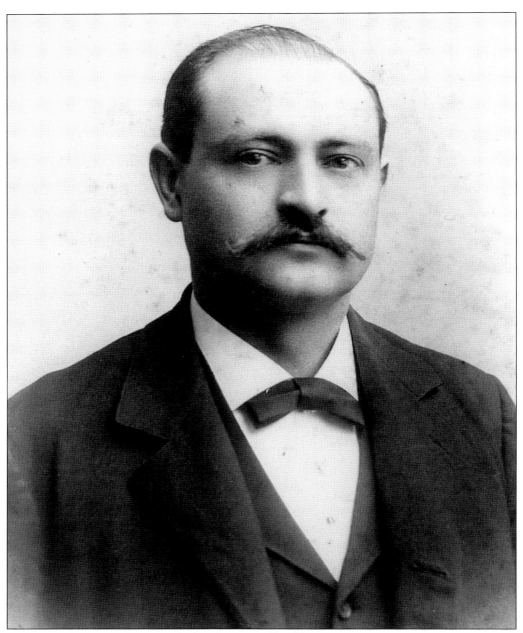

Peter Luger (1866–1941) is entombed in Cypress Hills Abbey. In 1887, Luger, a German immigrant, opened a steak house that to this day remains one of the most premier steak houses in America. Located in Williamsburg, Brooklyn, Luger became famous and wealthy by serving a simple menu of steak or chops, french-fried potatoes, onion-and-tomato salad, and beer and coffee. The scrubbed-oak tables, chairs, and bar added to the "no-frills" atmosphere. Customers flocked to Peter Luger's, not for atmosphere, but to simply eat steak. Luger, known for his serious demeanor, was present almost every evening. He would greet customers politely, but a smile was rare. According to Luger's obituary from the *Herald Tribune*, whether the customer was a Supreme Court Justice, baseball player, visiting notable from Hollywood, or famished steak lover from Wall Street, they were all the same to him.

James Watson (1826–1871) served as county auditor and key bookkeeper throughout the entire Boss Tweed corruption scandal. Watson was the ring's paymaster and was responsible for paying all illegal kickbacks to ring members and their associates. Ironically, when Watson unexpectedly died, his wife, Margaret, was forced to pay back his ill-gotten wealth, which amounted to $588,000 in 1876. He is buried in Section 14.

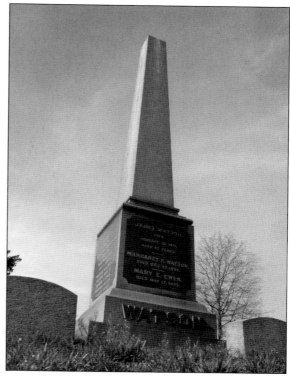

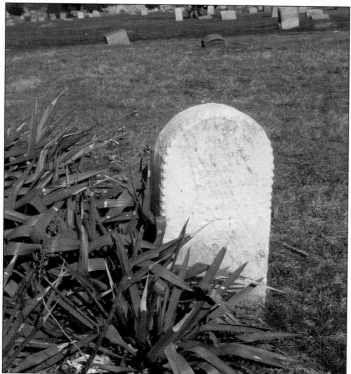

George H. Mills (1843–1885) holds the unfortunate distinction of being one of the few men to be sentenced to death by the State of New York. Pleading insanity, Mills's court case over the stabbing murder of his wife was 19th-century high drama. Mills strongly felt that the examining doctor and his acting attorney were all against him, which led to his execution. Mills was led to the gallows where onlookers witnessed his hanging. His body was immediately transported to Cypress Hills for interment in Locust Grove.

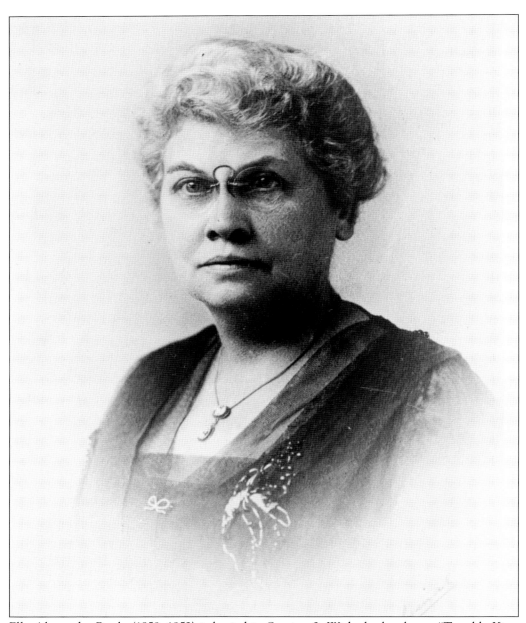

Ella Alexander Boole (1859–1952) is buried in Section 2. With the battle cry "Tremble King Alcohol! We Shall Grow Up!" Boole became a prominent figure for the Prohibition movement over the course of 40 years. She served as president of the New York, national, and world branch of the Women's Christian Temperance Union. In 1920, Boole was a candidate for the U.S. Senate on the Prohibition Party ticket opposing Republican senator J. W. Wadsworth. Although she lost, she received the largest number of votes of any woman running for public office up to that time; however, due to her fearless crusade against the evils of alcohol, she was successful in pressuring the U.S. Congress to pass the 18th (Prohibition) Amendment. Unfortunately, the Temperance Union's tragic hour came on June 30, 1933, when the 18th Amendment was repealed. Boole died of a stroke at age 93. (Courtesy of Library of Congress.)

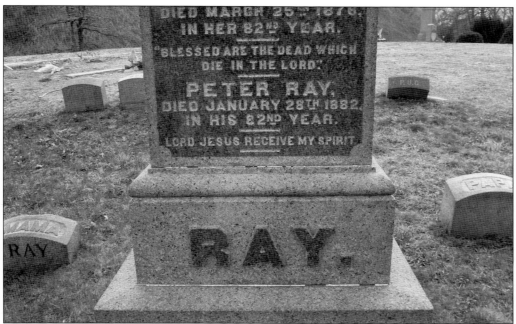

DIED MARCH 25 1876.
IN HER 82ND YEAR.
"BLESSED ARE THE DEAD WHICH
DIE IN THE LORD."
PETER RAY,
DIED JANUARY 28TH 1882.
IN HIS 82ND YEAR.
LORD JESUS RECEIVE MY SPIRIT

RAY.

Dr. Peter W. Ray (1800–1882) is interred in Section 11. Born in Brooklyn, Dr. Ray was both a practitioner of medicine and a pharmacist. For more than 55 years he was the proprietor of his own highly successful pharmacy. He also served as treasurer of the Brooklyn College of Pharmacy during the entirety of its existence up to the time of his death. Dr. Ray was well respected and recognized as a natural leader among his people. He enjoyed a large practice, and his patients came from some of Brooklyn's finest families.

James McCune Smith (1813–1865) was an American physician, apothecary, active abolitionist, and gifted writer. He holds the distinction of being the first African American to earn a medical degree and run a pharmacy in the United States. Smith wrote passionately about race stereotypes, intelligence, and society in general. His close friends included fellow abolitionist Frederick Douglas. Smith died just 19 days before the adoption of the 13th Amendment to the Constitution, abolishing slavery throughout the United States. He is interred in Section 2. (Courtesy of New York Public Library.)

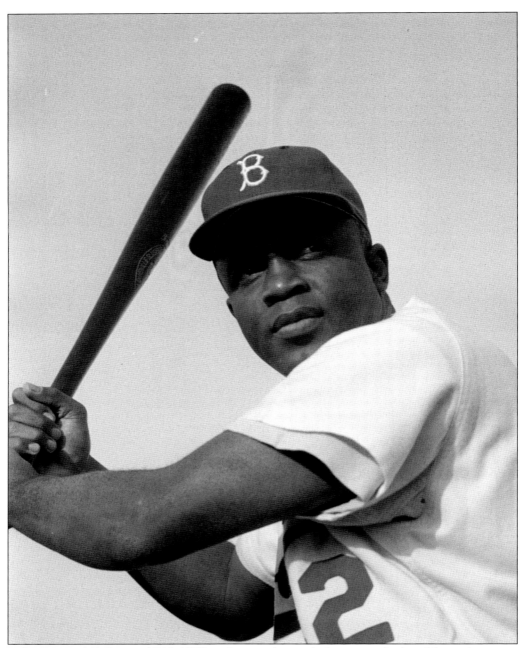

Jackie Roosevelt Robinson (1919–1972) made sports history by becoming the first African American to break the color barrier and play in modern Major League Baseball. A second basemen for the Brooklyn Dodgers, Robinson batted a career .311 along with being a daring base runner. In 1962, Robinson was elected into the Baseball Hall of Fame as the first black player to receive this honor. After leaving baseball, he became a vice president of a popular restaurant chain and served as special assistant of civil rights under Gov. Nelson Rockefeller of New York. Unfortunately, Robinson died young at age 53 from complications of diabetes. In 1997, his uniform number (42) was retired throughout Major League Baseball. He is buried in Section 6. (Courtesy of Library of Congress.)

Gavin Cato (1983–1991) of Brooklyn was just nine years old when he was struck and killed by a car on a hot August night in 1991. A Hasidic Jewish man who was believed to have run the red light in trying to keep up with a three-car motorcade hit him. The community was outraged at the mistreatment of Cato and the favoritism shown toward the driver. This tragedy set off a three-day outburst, the Crown Heights Riots, which became one of the most memorable clashes in New York City history. He is buried in Section 1.

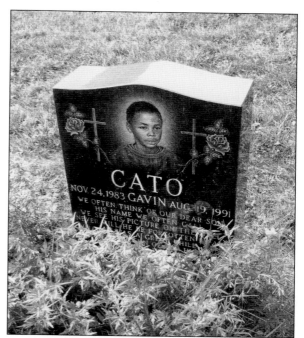

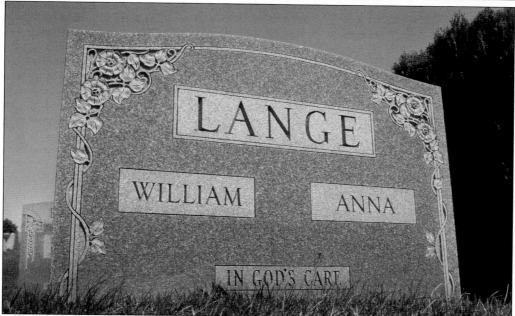

William Lange was an innovative pioneer in banjo making from 1897 until 1939. He is famous for his signature "Paramount" line of banjos, which were mainly professional-grade tenors that were inlaid and decorated. These highly specialized banjos were world famous for their piano volume and harp-quality tone. Lange was the sole owner of his state-of-the-art banjo factory, which had 250 workmen involved in every stage of banjo construction. Lange banjo manufacturing ceased in 1939, making Lange-style banjos highly collectible and very expensive. He is interred in Section 15.

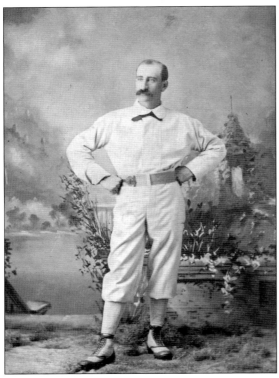

Robert Vagasour Ferguson (1845–1894), a native of Brooklyn, was an early-day baseball player, manager, and umpire before and after baseball became professional. In the early 1870s, he played for two fabled semiprofessional clubs, the New York Mutual's and the Brooklyn Atlantics. Nicknamed "Death to Flying Things," derived from his greatness as a defensive player, Ferguson appeared in 562 games with a lifetime batting average of .271. He is accredited with being the first documented batter to switch hit. He is buried in Section 4. (Courtesy of New York Public Library.)

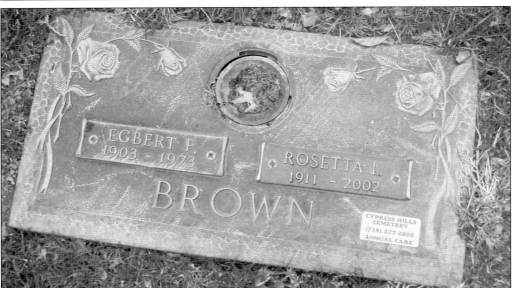

Rosetta L. Brown (1911–2002) is interred in Section 15. Born Rosetta Olive Burton in New York City, Brown was a stage, screen, and television actress. In film, she is best known for her role as a nurse in Neil Simon's *The Sunshine Boys*. Although Brown was an accomplished stage and film actress, it was television that made her a star. She was featured in several popular sitcoms including *Amen* and *Gimme a Break!* but is best known for her role as the sweet Estelle Winslow on the long-running sitcom *Family Matters*.

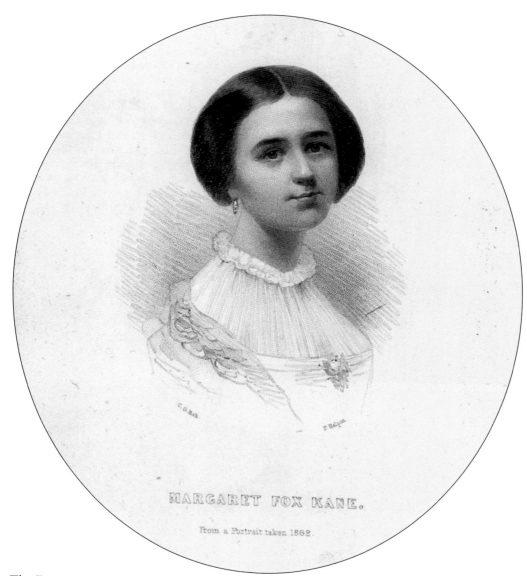

MARGARET FOX KANE.

From a Portrait taken 1862.

The Fox sisters, Margaret "Maggie" (1833–1893) and Kate (1837–1892), are buried in Section 3. During the 1800s no spiritual mediums were more illustrious or more celebrity than Margaret (pictured) and Kate Fox. In a century when mortality figures ran high, many people turned to spiritual mediums with hopeful hearts seeking to connect one last time with a deceased child or spouse. By 1850, the Fox sisters were popular for their public séances, attracting such notables as William Cullen Bryant, Sojourner Truth, Horace Greely, and even James Fenimore Cooper. Yet with all their séance success, there was always criticism. Their spiritual practices were considered frivolous and fake, filled with creative trickery. Unfortunately, the pressure and constant demand to perform led the sisters to heavy drinking. During a desperate time in 1888, Margaret was paid $1,500 to publicly appear at the New York Academy of Music and reveal, to an audience of over 2,000, her spiritual secrets, discrediting her and her sister's special abilities. Within five years of the confession, Kate died an alcoholic at 55 years of age. Margaret followed her sister's fate one year later, dying penniless and alone at age 60. (Courtesy of Joe Fodor.)

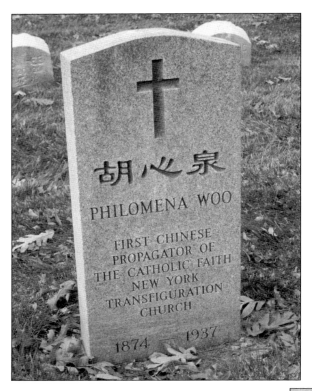

Philomena Woo (1874–1937), Chinatown's version of Mother Theresa, made history by becoming the first Chinese Catholic propagator of the Roman Catholic Transfiguration Church. Revered by the community as "Mother of Mercy," she worked tirelessly with several charities and provided constant care to the needy children of Chinatown for years. She taught English and the Roman Catholic religion all the way up to her untimely death. She is interred in Section 16.

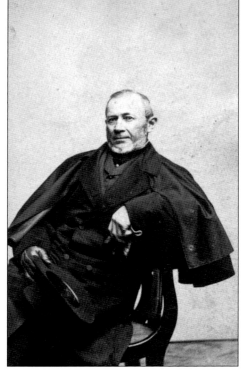

Hiram Woodruff (1817–1867) is buried in Section 6. During the golden age of horse racing at the Union Course Racetrack in Woodhaven, there was not one person, no horse trainer or horse driver, who stood out more than Woodruff. Following family tradition, young Woodruff was taught by his father, John, and his uncle, George, how to ride. His first race was in 1836 on the horse "Paul Pry." Woodruff died at the young age of 50. Along with him died the golden days of the Union Course Racetrack. (Courtesy of New York Public Library.)

Mary L. Booth (1831–1889) was the original editor in chief of the highly successful *Harper's Bazaar* from its founding in 1867 up until her death in 1889. Before her *Bazaar* editorial career, she wrote the *History of the City of New York* in 1859, which evolved into 11 illustrated volumes. This fascinating woman was an ardent abolitionist who was fluent in seven languages. She worked closely with Susan B. Anthony and Elizabeth Cady Stanton for women's equal rights. She is interred in Section 6. (Courtesy of Yaphank Historical Society.)

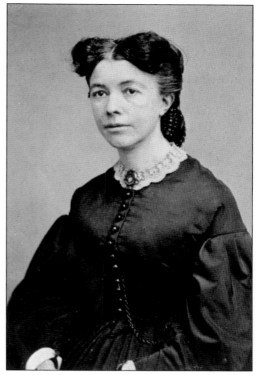

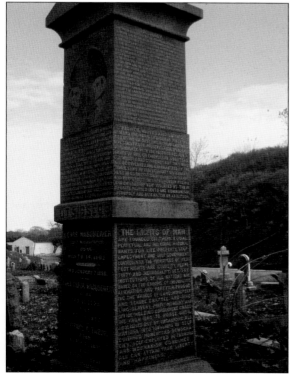

Lewis Masquerier (1802–1888) is buried in Section 9. His grave marker is as curious as the man buried beneath it. Masquerier was a highly acclaimed libertarian who held strong opinions on land ownership, society structure, and controlled government. Inscribed all over the 11-foot marble monument are Masquerier's wordy philosophies, odd markings, and secret symbols. It includes his most noted work "Sociology." Masquerier was also a pioneer in phonetic spelling and invented his own universal alphabet of 11 vowels and 22 consonants, which are also included on his grave marker.

89

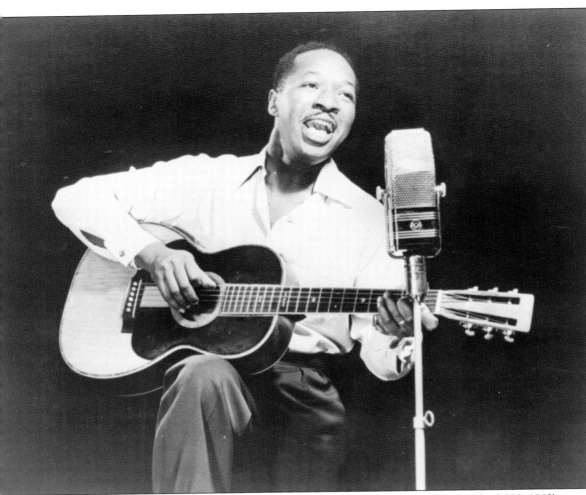

Joshua White (1914–1969) is interred in Section 18. Throughout the course of four decades (1920–1960), White was one of the world's most successful black entertainers. In the 1920s, he was the leading blues singer around the South and became the youngest soloist in the "race records" market. In the 1930s, he achieved recognition as a blues star, influencing a generation of southern players. In the 1940s, he discovered his white New York audience shifting to folk music. His recording of "One Meatball" was a folk-pop smash, and he became the only black guitarist to have his own national tour. In the 1950s, White toured Europe and became a star in England. During the early 1960s, the folk-revival had hit, and by 1963, he was ranked as America's third most-popular folk singer. White's health began to rapidly decline in the early 1960s due to being a lifelong smoker. While surgeons were attempting a new medical procedure to replace his heart valves, the surgery failed; at age 55, White died on the operating table. (Courtesy of Library of Congress.)

Henry W. Meyer (1850–1898) was born in Germany and came to America in 1864. In 1871, young Meyer purchased a failing grocery, curtailed credit to customers, and expanded one of the stores sidelines, selling tobacco at wholesale prices to retailers. As sales increased, Meyer established his own tobacco factory in Williamsburg—the Ivanhoe Brand Pipe and Chewing Tobacco Company. In 1890, he moved his factory to Glendale, New York, only to sell it four years later to the American Tobacco Company, making him very wealthy. He is buried in Restmount 1.

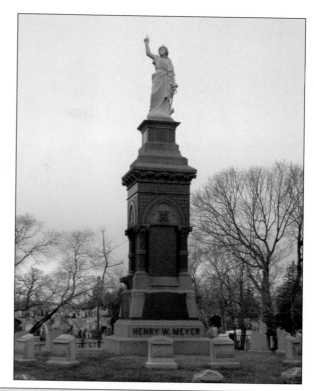

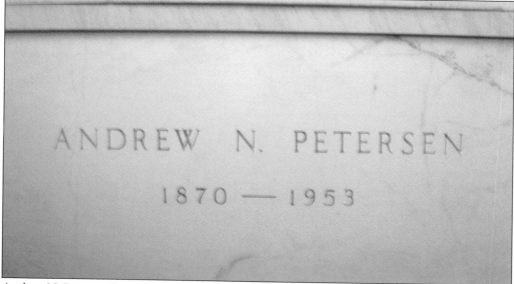

Andrew N. Petersen (1870–1953) is entombed in Cypress Hills Abbey. Born in Denmark, Petersen was three years old when his parents immigrated to America. As a young man, Petersen learned the pattern maker's trade and eventually became president of the largest foundry—the Brooklyn Foundry Company. At 51, Petersen entered politics and became a U.S. Representative from New York and served the 67th Congress from March 4, 1921, through March 3, 1923. In 1922, he ran an unsuccessful reelection, so he returned to his original vocation.

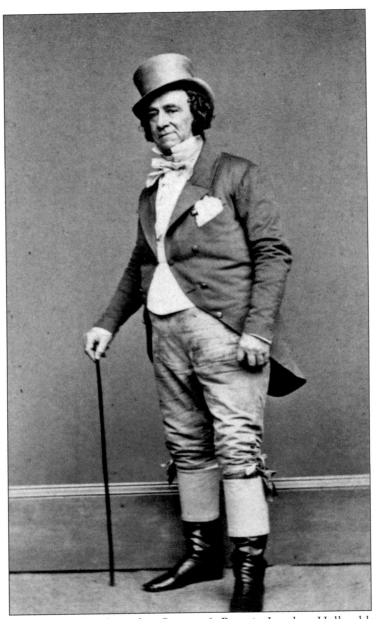

George Holland (1791–1870) is buried in Section 6. Born in London, Holland became one of the early pioneers in stage acting and dedicated over 50 years of his life to playing hundreds of characters in England and the United States. Part vagabond, part nomad, Holland performed in England until he came to New York in 1827. He debuted at the Bowery Theatre in *A Day After the Fair,* then a favorite farce, which he made into a popular hit. Holland later traveled from city to city, acting in Boston, Louisville, Montgomery, and Providence, without making much money. His most profitable years were 1835 to 1842 at the St. Charles Theatre in New Orleans, where he acted alongside Charlotte Cushman in *Rob Roy* and *Lady Macbeth.* "God bless you" were his last words spoken on stage at a benefit play, *Frou-Frou.* These same words are inscribed on his simple headstone.

Five

MEMORIALS AND HONORS EARNED

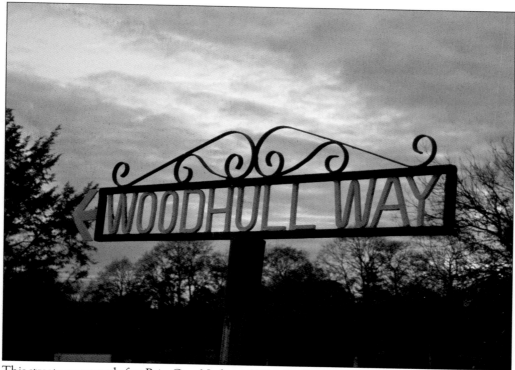

This street was named after Brig. Gen. Nathaniel Woodhull, who served under George Washington during the War of Independence. Woodhull was responsible for preparing the militia to help repel the British invasion of New York. A key player during the Battle of Long Island, Woodhull was eventually captured by British troops and subsequently died of injuries. He is buried in the Woodhull family burial ground in Mastic Beach, Long Island.

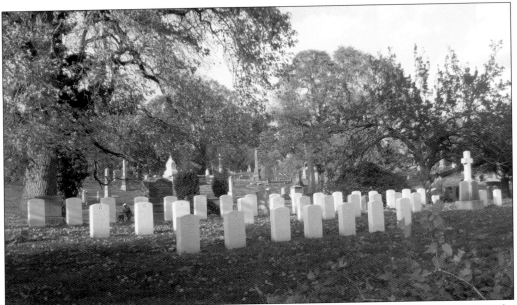

Near the main entrance, a section named the Mount of Victory plot is the final resting place for 39 soldiers who served in the War of 1812. The first interment was made on June 10, 1854. Isaac Daniels, who served in both the Revolutionary War and the War of 1812, is buried here. This 2,500-square-foot section has the distinction of being the smallest parcel of federally owned land in the country.

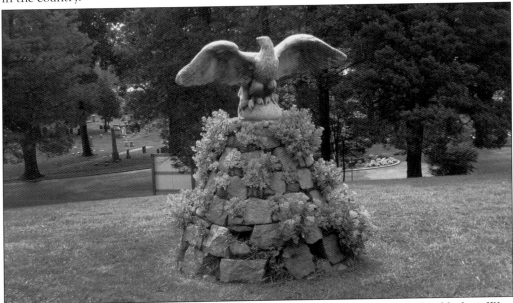

Situated inside the Mount of Victory plot is the eye-catching Eagle Monument. Visible from West Dolorosa Road, the eagle is perched on top of a 6-foot pyramid of rough fieldstones. Constructed by Cypress Hill's laborers in 1934, the large stone eagle with a 4.5-foot wingspan was sculpted atop the pyramid by the Londino Construction Company in the Bronx, New York. Eagles symbolize courage and communicate military action during one's life.

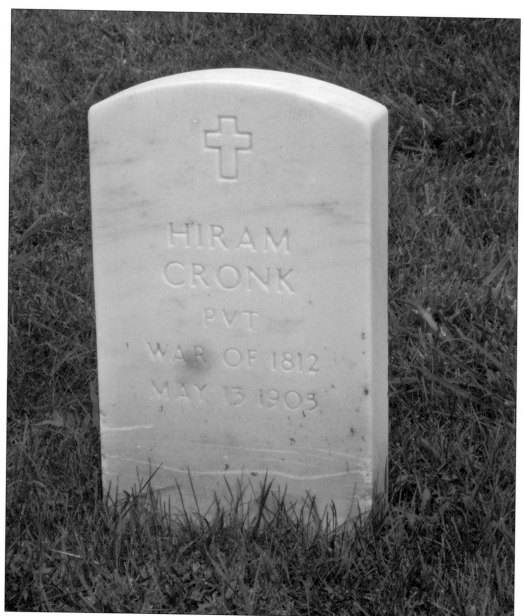

When Pvt. Hiram Cronk (1800–1903) entered the world at the dawn of 19th century, he could never have imagined the unique accolade accredited to him at the end of his long life. Born in Frankfort, New York, Cronk, at 14 years of age, enlisted with the U.S. Army along with his father and two brothers on August 4, 1814. He served with the New York Volunteers in the defense of Sacketts Harbor, where he defended his country for about 100 days. Cronk's adult life was spent as a shoemaker supporting a large family. He was blessed with a long life, living to be 103 years of age. When Cronk died in 1903, he made history as the last surviving veteran of the War of 1812. His funeral was a huge public event, drawing thousands to pay their respects as his body laid in state at New York's city hall. At the cemetery, Cronk was buried according to traditional Grand Army ritual in the Mount of Victory plot.

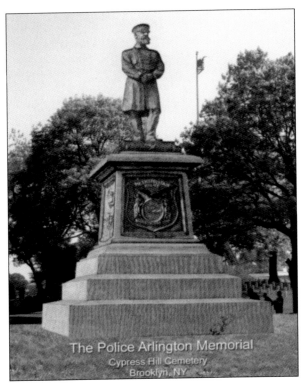

The Police Arlington Memorial
Cypress Hill Cemetery
Brooklyn, NY

In 1871, this 7.5-foot bronze statue of Metropolitan Police officer Lester Lewis was placed on a 10-foot stone pedestal. For 94 years, officer Lewis stood at Parade Rest with hands joined in front watching over his fallen comrades who were interred in the Police Arlington Memorial. Unexpectedly in 1966, the statue of Lester was stolen in the middle of the night. This was a remarkable feat considering that Lester weighed over 2,000 pounds. To this day, he has not been recovered; however, there is a replacement statue in the progress. (Courtesy of Cypress Hills Cemetery Archives.)

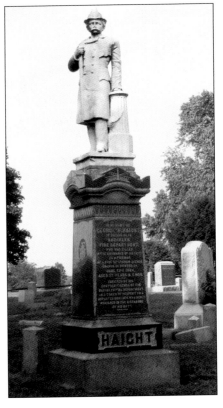

In 1884, George Haight and Lt. Jonathan Tyack, both of Ladder 6, were ordered to add another section of hose to the waterline operating in the rear of a bakery located on Graham Avenue at the corner of Powers Street in Brooklyn when the brick wall of the burning bakery collapsed on them. The inscription on the monument states the following: "Erected by the brother firemen of the Brooklyn Fire Department as a token of respect to their departed brothers who nobly perished in the line of duty."

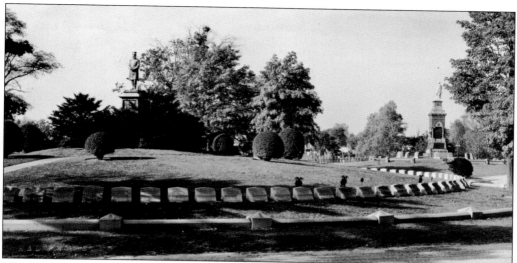

The first police memorial of its kind created in the United States, the Police Arlington Memorial was established in 1871 by the Metropolitan Police Benevolent Association. With only 89 interments to date, the memorial was designed to be a place of pride and to honor the bravery of police officers. One of the last policemen to find a resting place here was Henry Hayward of the Rough Riders. He fell in the charge at San Juan Hill and was identified by the police shield pinned to his uniform. (Courtesy of Cypress Hills Cemetery Archives.)

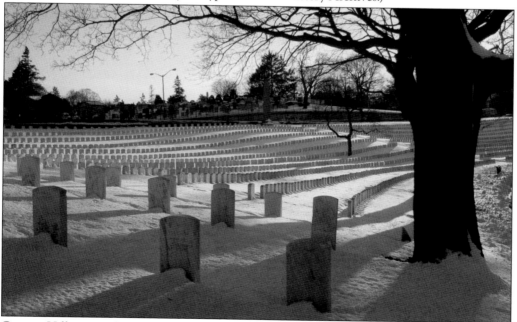

Cypress Hills is privileged to be one of the select few cemeteries in the United States to have a national cemetery situated within its grounds. In 1862, a 3.5-acre section was designated a military burial ground for 7,000 Union soldiers of the American Civil War. In 1941, the bodies of 235 Confederate prisoners were interred here. Excluding Arlington National Cemetery and the Battlefield Cemetery at Gettysburg, this plot holds more dead from the Gettysburg battle than any other cemetery in the country.

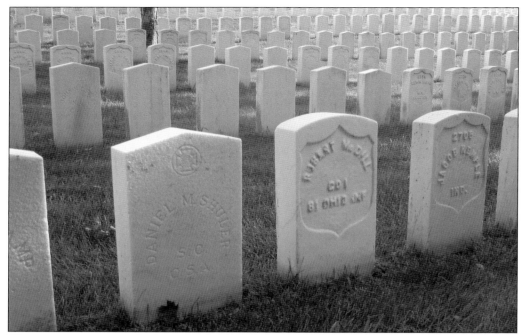

These government-issued white monoliths identify the fallen veterans of the Civil War. At left in the first row is Daniel M. Shuler, a Confederate soldier from South Carolina. To the right of Shuler is Union soldier Robert McDill of Ohio. The top of Shuler's headstone is peaked, identifying him as a Confederate soldier, while McDill's is rounded to signify a Union soldier. This is a standard feature in all national cemeteries.

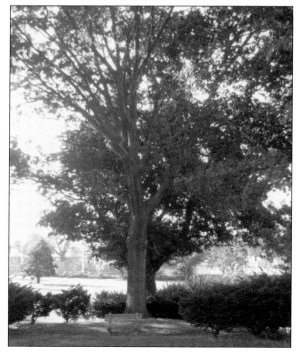

On November 3, 1881, within the national cemetery section of Cypress Hills, the James A. Garfield Oak Society of Brooklyn planted an oak tree in honor of the slain 20th president of the United States. For several years, an ornate wrought-iron fence encircled the memorial tree. Inscribed on the fence was the following: "James A. Garfield shot July 2, 1881, and James A. Garfield died September 19, 1881." The tree and the fence (now gone) was the first memorial in the United States to honor Garfield.

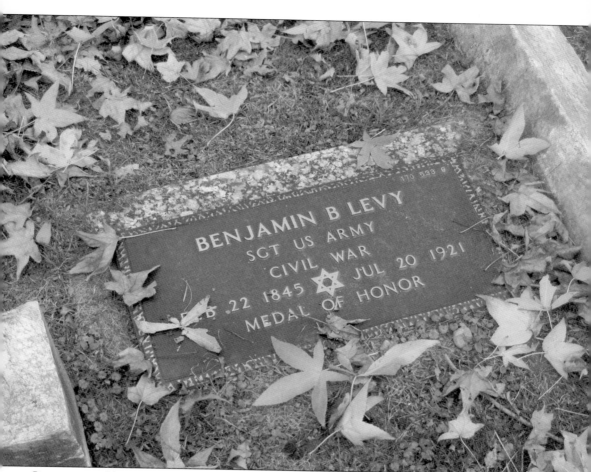

BENJAMIN B LEVY
SGT US ARMY
CIVIL WAR
FEB 22 1845 ✡ JUL 20 1921
MEDAL OF HONOR

Sixteen-year-old Benjamin B. Levy (1845–1921) voluntarily enlisted in the First New York Infantry as a drummer boy. Drummers and color (flag) bearers were essential to battlefield communication and were placed at the front lines to lead the regiment into intense battle, easily being the first to be killed. Seeing the colors held high was a crucial guide. If the color bearer was killed, the regiment could easily become confused and disoriented. After several minutes of brutal fighting, the color bearer was cut down and killed. Private Levy jumped forward and picked up the colors, waving and holding them high to inspire the First Infantry of New York. The line stabilized and rallied around the battle flag due to Levy's gallantry. As a result of his extraordinary bravery in the line of fire, Levy was promoted to sergeant and awarded the Medal of Honor. Additionally, Sergeant Levy made history by being the first Jewish recipient of the Medal of Honor on March 1, 1865.

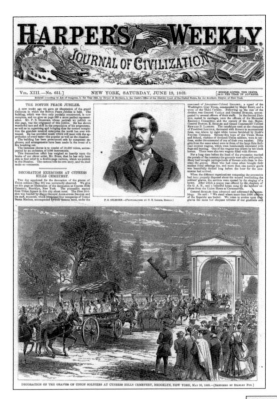

HARPER'S WEEKLY

JOURNAL OF CIVILIZATION

This detailed illustration appeared in *Harper's Weekly* in 1869, depicting a parade-like procession entering the gates of Cypress Hills Cemetery during the decoration of the graves of Union soldiers. Today this tribute is called Memorial Day. At left, sketch artist Stanley Fox depicts the spouses of the deceased seated in an Erie Canal Railroad Express wagon drawn by 10 elaborately decorated horses. (Courtesy of Cypress Hills Cemetery Archives.)

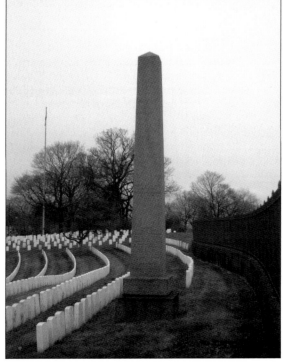

This large 25-foot-tall obelisk perched on the southwest ridge of Section 1B in the national cemetery of Cypress Hills is the Ringgold Monument. Erected by the veteran officers and soldiers who proudly served under the command of 103rd Maj. Benjamin Ringgold during the Civil War, this memorial was unveiled in 1878.

The Tomb of the Unknown Soldier in Arlington National Cemetery is a sobering tribute that thousands of visitors pay homage to every year; however, in national cemeteries across the country, there are several single tablature markers that read, "Unknown U.S. Soldier." This is just one of the many disturbing realities of war. The identities of brave men and women who fought and died for our freedom are sometimes lost in the process.

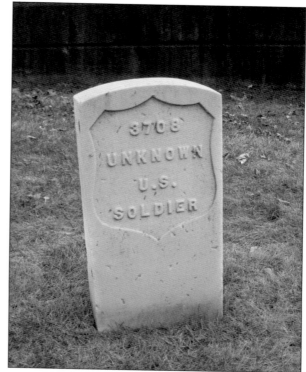

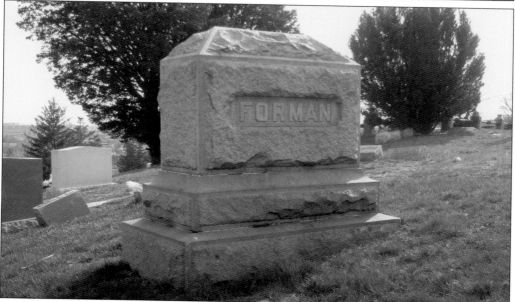

Nineteen-year-old Cpl. Alexander Forman (1843–1922) was one of the nine men awarded the Medal of Honor for heroism during a two-day engagement with Confederate forces at Fair Oaks, Virginia, on May 31 and June 1, 1862. On May 31, Corporal Forman was wounded but ignored his pain and loss of blood in order to continue to fight until he fainted and had to be carried off the battlefield.

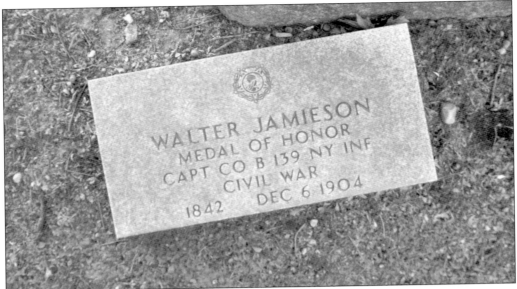

First Sgt. Walter Jamieson (1842–1904) was awarded the Medal of Honor for two separate acts of bravery during the Civil War. On July 30, 1864, Jamieson voluntarily rushed between enemy lines to assist a wounded and helpless officer whom he carried for over 400 yards safely back to Union lines. He was cited again for his heroism at Fort Harrison, Virginia, on September 29 when he seized the regimental color from the fallen color bearer. He rushed and planted the colors upon the fort.

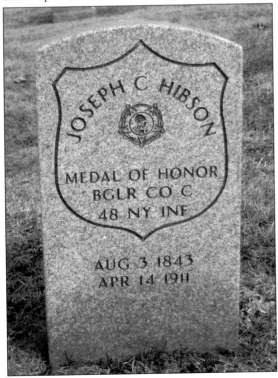

Pvt. Joseph C. Hibson (1843–1911), a 20-year-old bugler, received the Medal of Honor for three separate acts of bravery. One such act occurred on July 13, 1863, during a bombardment of Fort Wagner, South Carolina. Hibson volunteered himself to fill in for a sick comrade. After midnight, rebels infiltrated and bayoneted Hibson's comrade on guard duty and demanded Private Hibson surrender. Hibson stood his ground and instead killed his attacker.

Thousands of gravestones accurately depict the names and dates of previous generations, but only one monument that bears a pen name is more famous then the real name above it. Gen. Charles G. Halpine's (1830–1868) name is on the large granite monument; however, near the bottom inscribed into the cold stone is the name "Miles O'Reilly." Halpine, a creative journalist in civilian life, enlisted in the 69th New York Infantry in 1861. During the Civil War, under the pseudonym Pvt. Miles O'Reilly, he began sending detailed letters to Abraham Lincoln, Secretary of War Edwin Stanton, General Grant, and even to the top brass of the navy, advising them on how to win the war. Letters from Private O'Reilly became so well known, and apparently abrasive to some, that the navy ordered him to be found and court-martialed. Halpine died at age 38 of an accidental drug overdose.

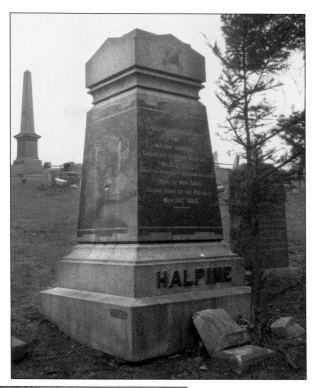

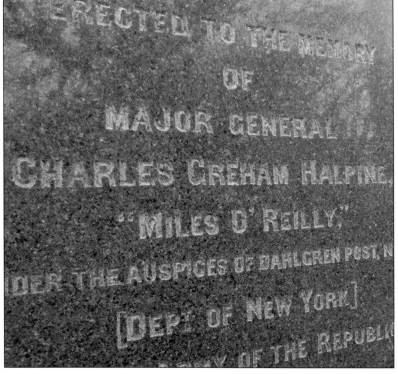

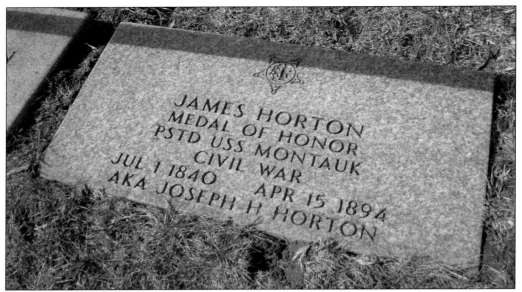

On the night of September 21, 1864, at Port Royal, South Carolina, a fire broke out in the magazine light room of the USS *Montauk*, causing panic and demoralizing the crew. Gunner's Mate James Horton (1840–1894) was one of three members of the ship's crew who remained alert to the deadly danger and earned the Medal of Honor. Horton rushed into the burning cabin, obtained the magazine keys, sprang into the light room, and began extinguishing all combustibles including the box of signals where the fire originated.

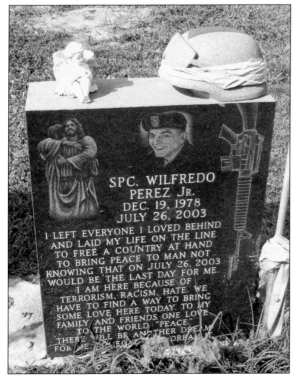

Proudly serving his country in Operation Iraqi Freedom as a mortarman in the First Battalion, 67th Armored Regiment, 4th Infantry Division, Spc. Wilfredo Perez Jr. (1978–2003) was guarding a children's hospital in Baqubah on July 26, 2003, when to the brave soldier's peril, war insurgents tossed grenades from the upper floors of the hospital, killing him. "Junior," as he was affectionately called by his family, received a Commendation, a Purple Heart, and a Bronze Star.

John G. Morrison (1842–1897) earned the Medal of Honor during the Civil War for his heroism on July 15, 1862, at Yazoo River, Mississippi. Serving onboard the USS *Carondelet*, Morrison was commended for his exemplary conduct and his brave actions during an engagement with the rebel ram vessel *Arkansas*. When the *Carondelet* was badly damaged, Morrison took control and called the boarders on deck and was the first to return to the guns and give the rebel ram a broadside, sinking it as it passed. He was rewarded with the Union Medal of Highest Honor.

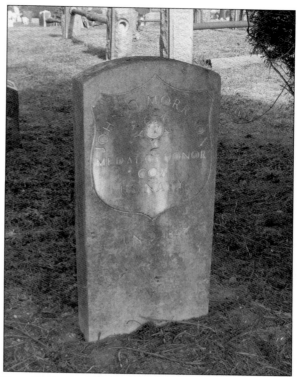

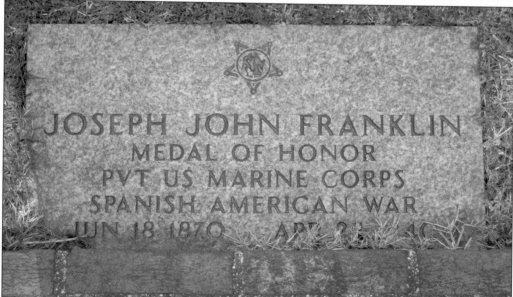

Pvt. Joseph John Franklin (1870–1940) earned the Medal of Honor during the Spanish-American War for heroism on May 11, 1898, at Cienfuegos, Cuba. Franklin was one of 52 sailors and marines cited for bravery and coolness in the face of fierce enemy fire during the cutting of undersea communication cables. Destruction of the cables was ordered to disrupt enemy communication with outside forces.

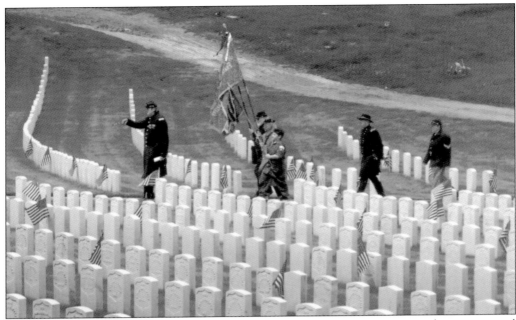

Every Memorial Day the Sons of Union Veterans of the Civil War come together in national cemeteries to remember our fallen heroes. This important organization was founded in 1881 as the successor to the Grand Army of the Republic and was chartered in 1954 by an Act of Congress. Each year a local chapter from Brooklyn, Oliver Tilden Camp No. 26, assembles in Cypress Hills for commemorative services. The camp's color guard and musical unit lead with marching, special tributes, and finally, flag placements. Scouts Andrew Duer (left) and Joseph Capuano from Troop 105, pictured below, honor war veterans each year by placing flags at the grave sites. (Above, courtesy of Patrick Russo; below, courtesy of *Daily News*.)

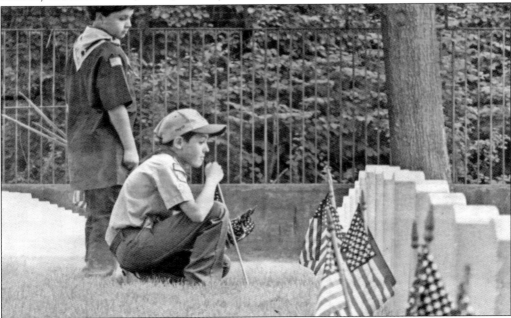

Six

Fellowship in Immortality

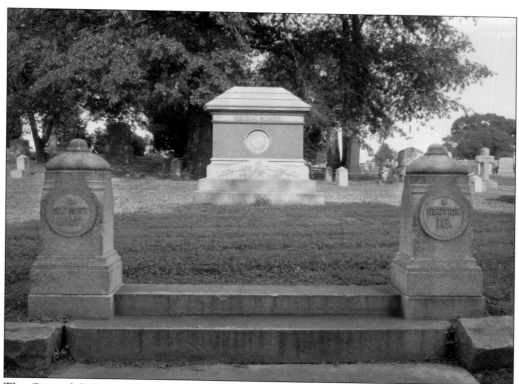

The General Society of Mechanics and Tradesmen of New York City has a 6,000-square-foot burial plot. The society was created in 1795 to provide cultural, educational, and social services to families of skilled craftsmen. In the middle of the plot is a three-tiered granite and polished-marble monument with a peaked top erected in 1963. Surprisingly there are only 23 people interred in the entire plot.

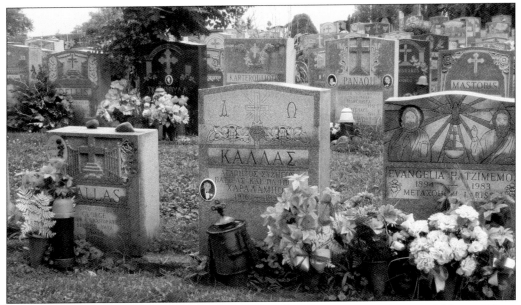

There are a large number of Greek headstones found in the appropriately named Mount Olives section of Cypress Hills. Most Greek headstones share a common symbol: the cross and a small oval portrait of the deceased on the face of the stone. Ornamental flowers and votive candles decorate the graves. The Greek culture is traditionally devoted to visiting grave sites of passed loved ones and friends.

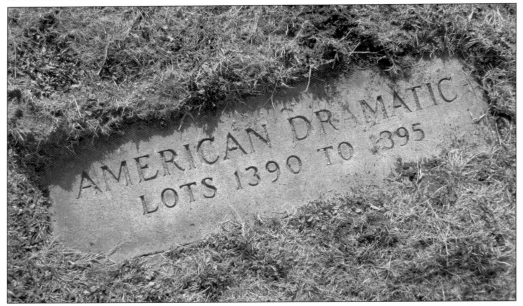

The American Dramatist Fund burial plot is a special place in Cypress Hills. Among the many working actors buried here, George Holland is especially memorable. The following is a memorable anecdote: "When his friend made arrangements for George's funeral at a Manhattan church and was told they do not bury actors but perhaps 'The Little Church Around the Corner' would do such a thing, his friend said, 'God Bless the Little Church.' " The name is still in use today.

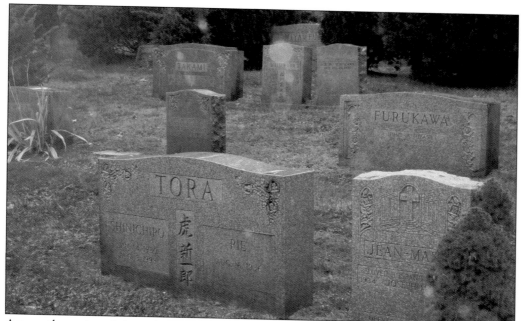

Among the various Asian cultures scattered throughout this great metropolis, the Japanese culture has embraced the American dream. Many have chosen to live, work, and even at the end, make Cypress Hills their final resting place. This Japanese section enhances the ethnic diversity of this historic cemetery.

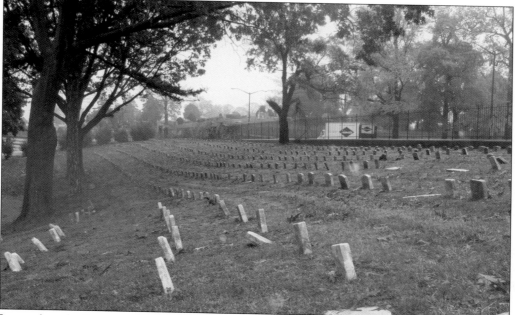

Located on the far western end of the cemetery bordering Cypress Hills Street is an area of small, white, simple gravestones. Some contain only a name, others only a number. These stones mark the remains of those persons who left their bodies for medical research at Mount Sinai Hospital located in Manhattan.

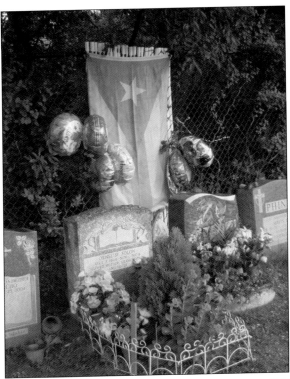

Hispanic culture is often represented in colorful grave displays featuring flowers, flags, balloons, and ceramic figures, such as crucifixes and angels. Many Puerto Rican grave sites reflect their exuberant attitude and zest for life. The Latin culture is well represented in the cemetery grounds.

One of the most striking obelisks in the cemetery is this tall, slender 25-foot monument, which is devoted to approximately 50 deceased New York Press Club members. Founded in 1948, the club is a professional organization of members in the news media. Its mission is to meet the needs and interests of professional journalists and to provide public service to the community. This club was originally called the New York Newspaper Reporters Association.

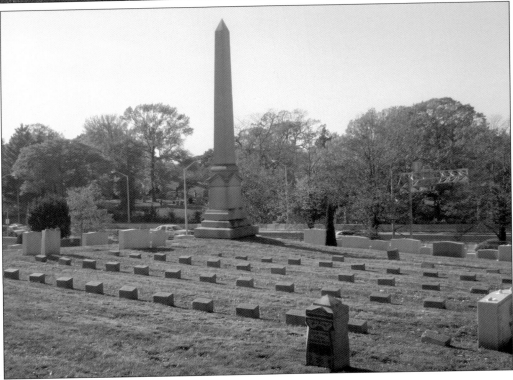

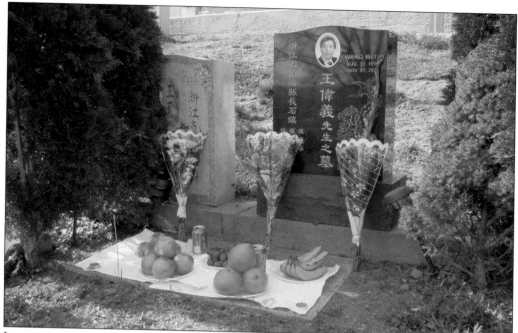

Large sections of Cypress Hills are the final resting places for the Chinese community. The Chinese have unique rituals that they have practiced for thousands of years. Relatives often place paper money as well as food on and around the grave so that the deceased will have sustenance to carry them on their long journey into the afterlife. Another common practice is the color of the characters of the living and deceased names inscribed on the headstone. The inscription of the living would be painted in white. When that individual died, the white color would be painted over in red. Every year in the spring, on April 5, the Chinese practice the Ching-Ming Festival. This is a special day when relatives clean around the grave, plant fresh flowers, and remember the dead.

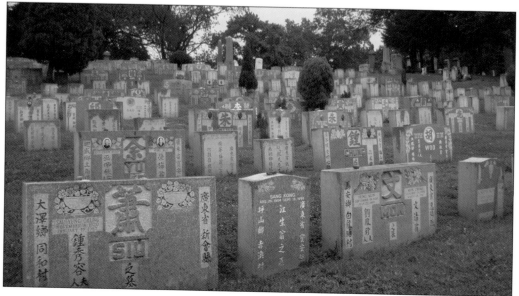

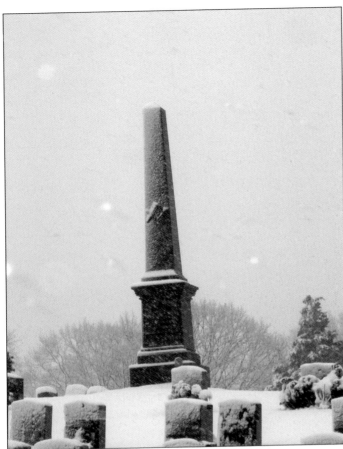

Prominently placed high on a hill in Maple View, the Masonic Order obelisk stands tall and proud. An extremely common stone monument, obelisks are of Egyptian influence. Obelisks are considered to be tasteful art forms associated with greatness and patriotism with pure, uplifting lines. At one time, local Masonic lodges were much more prominent then they are today. One of the main focuses of Freemasonry is charity and community service activity.

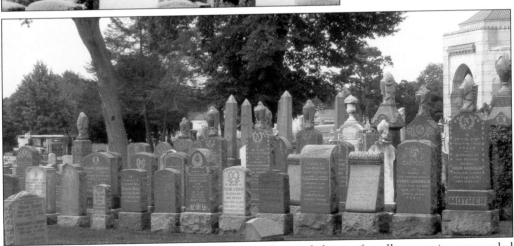

The cemetery founders looked upon their land as a fraternal cluster of small cemeteries surrounded by one common enclosure. Every religious organization, lodge, and benevolent society was allowed to consecrate their own grounds according to its own rites and customs. Unlike non-Jewish graves that accommodate multiple burials, Jewish religious law allows only one body per grave. This explains why many Jewish headstones are situated very close to one another.

Situated on a 1-acre circular plot of land, this large brown-granite monument is in memory of the Cannon Street Baptist Church members whose bodies were removed from the churchyard in Brooklyn and reinterred here between 1874 and 1875. Over the years Cypress Hills Cemetery has provided numerous acres of land for reinterments that came from Brooklyn and Manhattan churchyards.

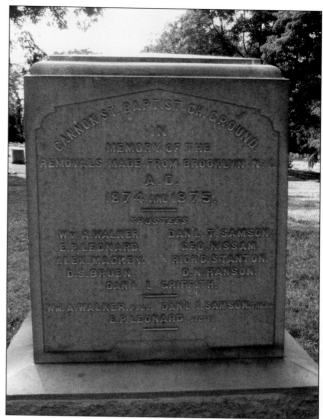

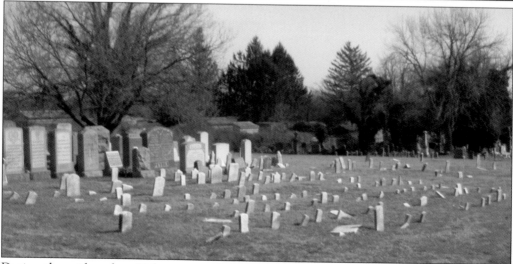

During the mid- to late 19th century, the infant mortality rate was 25 percent of all infants born into the inner city environment. Poverty, dreadful housing, and unhealthy urban sanitary conditions contributed to a wide variety of diseases that were incurable during this harsh time. The large number of small tablet markers that dot the Cypress Hills landscape reflect this painful period. Many died so long ago that the markers are completely illegible.

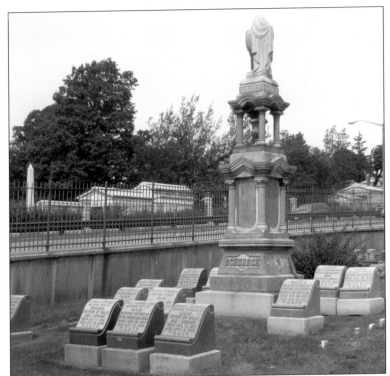

This large impressive granite monument is in eternal memory of the Schorsch family. The detailed stonework is surmounted by a draped funerary urn symbolizing death. The formal burial setting consists of granite footstones with scrolled tops containing names, dates, and Hebrew inscriptions. Directly across the street is the Salem Fields Jewish Cemetery. The Schorsch family members, buried in Cypress Hills, are as close as one can get to Salem Fields without actually being there.

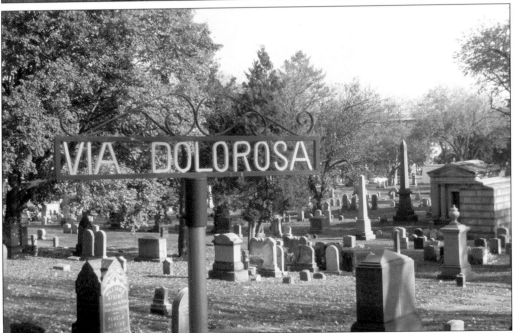

Latin for "the way of grief" or "way of suffering," Via Dolorosa is the street in Jerusalem that Jesus walked carrying his cross on the way to his crucifixion. This is the main roadway, which leads from the entrance gate northward to the once-existing receiving tomb.

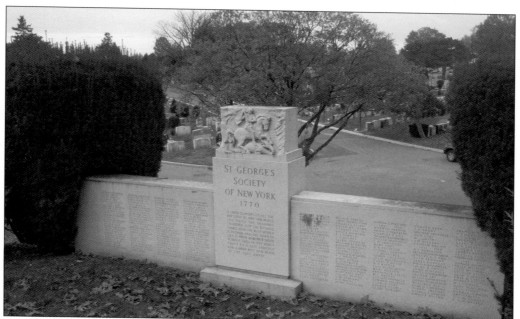

The St. George Society monument contains a listing of deceased society members, along with a carving of St. George with a shield fighting off a dragon. The society was founded by Englishmen living in New York in 1770. Its mission is to assist fellow countrymen in distress. St. George is the patron saint of England.

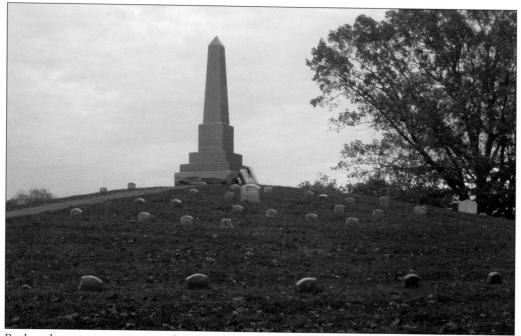

Rather than a monument, an obelisk marks the plot of deceased St. Andrew Society members. This four-tiered granite obelisk is placed atop a knoll with small footstones encircling it. St. Andrew is the patron saint of Scotland.

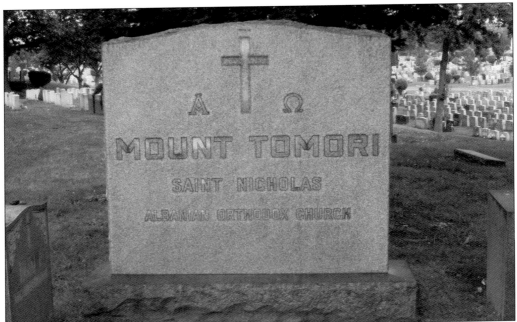

In the Albanian Orthodox section, the main stone is inscribed "Mount Tomori," named for one of the highest peaks in southern Albania. This peak is a huge, natural, isolated fortress and a sacred site for pilgrims. The neighboring countries of Albania and Greece are once again near each other in death, as the grave stones to the right are part of the Greek section. The Greek letters Alpha and Omega on the stone symbolize the beginning and the end.

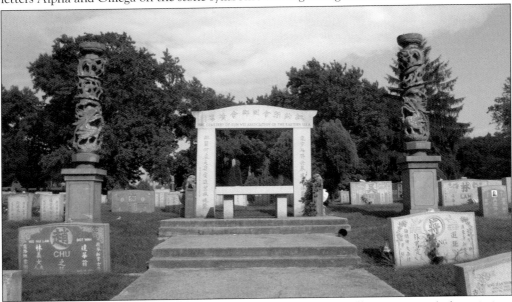

Located in a part of Section 16 are the graves of the Sun Wei Small Businessmen's Association. The grounds feature a carved bench for resting visitors, foo dogs placed for protection, and two intricately carved symbolic columns, which create a vertical counterpoint to an otherwise flat landscape.

Seven

TODAY AND TOMORROW

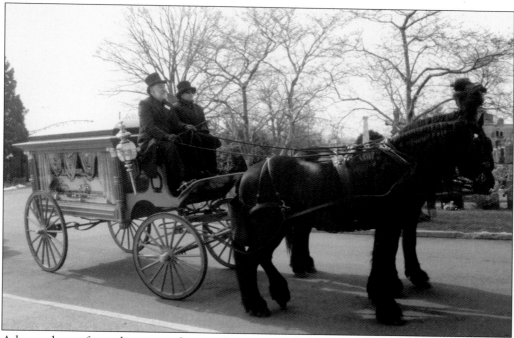

A horse-drawn funeral carriage elevates the level of honor and distinction to a funeral and is a memorable way to pay tribute to the deceased. The glass-enclosed carriage, adorned with period lanterns and drapery, quietly enters the grounds pulled by two black horses and driven by two solemn drivers dressed in black. The carriage slowly proceeds to the grave site with family and friends following behind. This historical-looking photograph was actually taken in 2010.

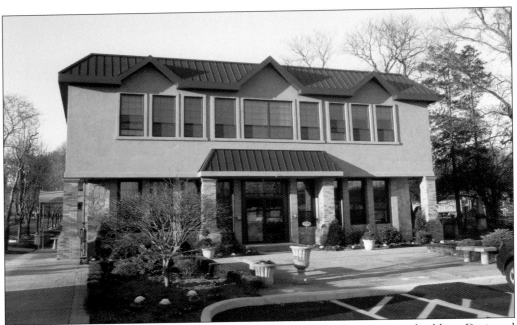

The most recent addition to the cemetery is the Cypress Hills administration building. Designed by local architect Gerard Caliendo, the structure was completed in October 2009. The building is highly functional and equipped with all modern amenities. The building contains large, bright offices and a state-of-the-art conference room.

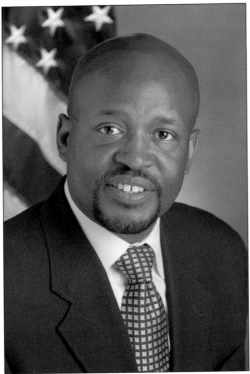

Darryl C. Towns shares his support of the Cypress Hills Cemetery: "As State Assemblyman of the 54th District, I proudly represent the Cypress Hills community. It is comforting and reassuring to know that our community is well served by the Cypress Hills Cemetery. Through the years they have provided the necessary burial needs in a professional, courteous, and respectful manner. I congratulate the Cypress Hills Cemetery staff for a job well done and wish them future success for many years to come."

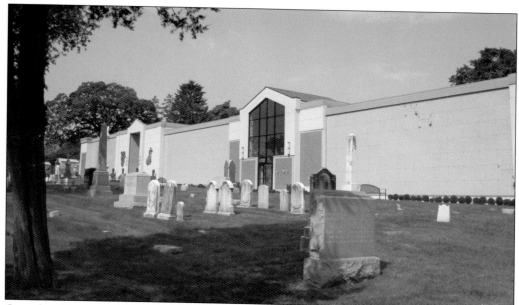

Completed in June 2008 at a cost of $3.5 million, the Melrose Memorial Garden mausoleum provides an alternative to inground interments. The facility features an indoor chapel, covered walkways, and stained glass. The community mausoleum offers 700 single crypts, 200 twin crypts (side by side), 340 tandem crypts (one behind the other), and 800 niches for cremated remains. All aboveground niches and crypts are constructed of beautiful and protective granite.

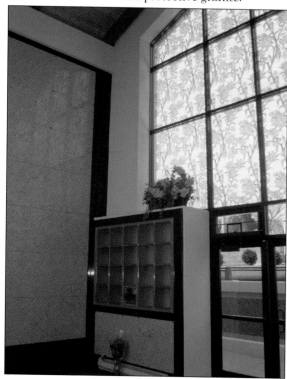

Located in the Melrose Memorial Garden mausoleum is a private chapel. A sun-drenched space adorned with high ceilings and stained glass in floral designs, the chapel offers 30 single crypts, 40 twin crypts, and 60 niches with bronze-etched glass.

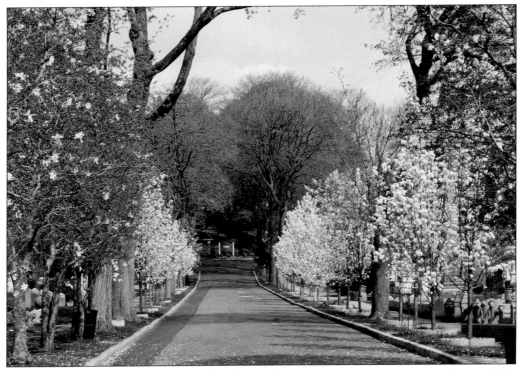

Lining both sides of Via Dolorosa and placed throughout the entire cemetery are the Cypress Hills memorial trees. The memorial tree program was established five years ago for the purchase of a young sapling dedicated in the memory of a past loved one. A silver plaque with the person's name is neatly placed at the base of the tree along with seasonal flowers. This successful program continues to beatify the grounds while remembering someone special in a unique and thoughtful way.

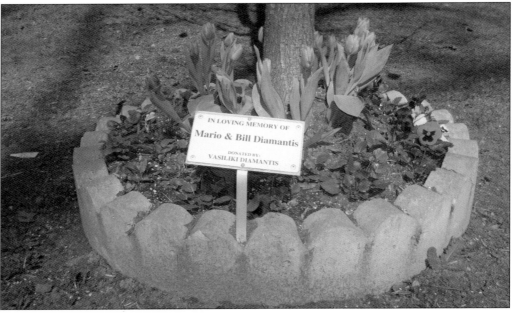

An important aspect of maintaining a historic cemetery is the ongoing restoration work. It is essential to keep the grounds looking their best, for this is a meaningful gesture of respect. One of the many responsibilities of the cemetery includes lifting and positioning headstones onto their original bases. This is not an easy task for it involves care, precision, balance, and strength. Pictured is a 5-foot-tall white sandstone monument that has fallen on the ground.

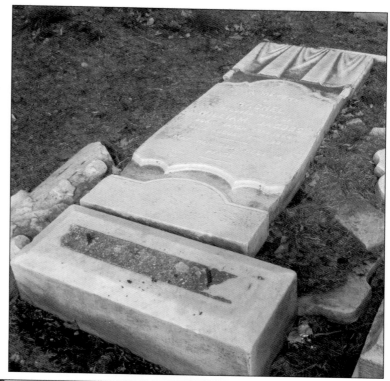

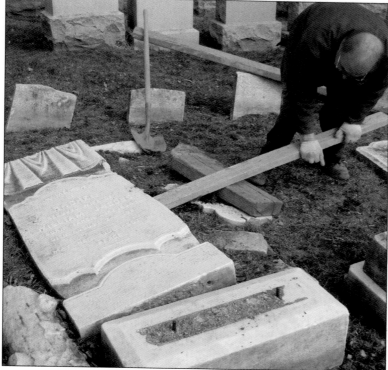

There are several areas within the grounds that are too crowded for machinery to enter and lift monuments. Here a staff member uses an ancient method of lifting by positioning a wood base under a wooden beam to act as a fulcrum in order to lift the heavy stone on its side.

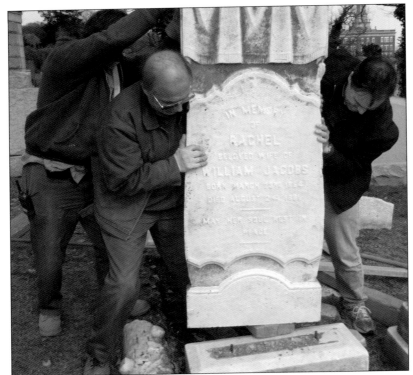

Considering the 500-pound-plus weight of this long, flat headstone, the positioning requires the strength of three men to upright the fallen monument. It must then be maneuvered up the wooden plank to be fitted onto the base.

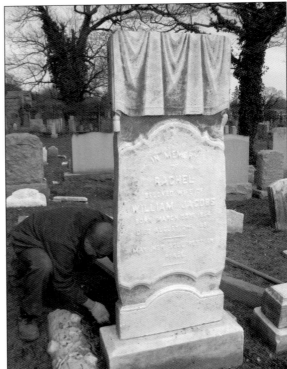

The monument is then positioned on its original base where it is aligned with two upright dowels. Monuments fall over due to age, severe weather conditions, and unfortunately, vandalism.

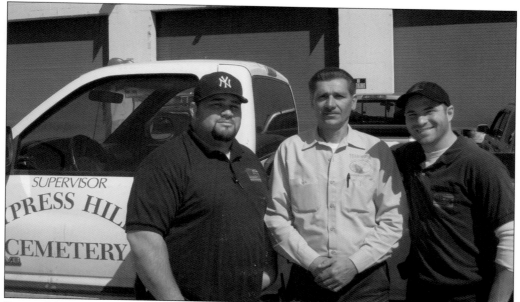

Pictured from left to right are Anthony Manero (10 years of service), Carmine DePrima (15 years of service), and Anthony Desmond (3 years of service). They are the three field supervisors at Cypress Hills. These men play important roles, for they oversee all cemetery operations including burials, ground maintenance, foundation pouring, and stone restoration. They manage a full-time staff year round.

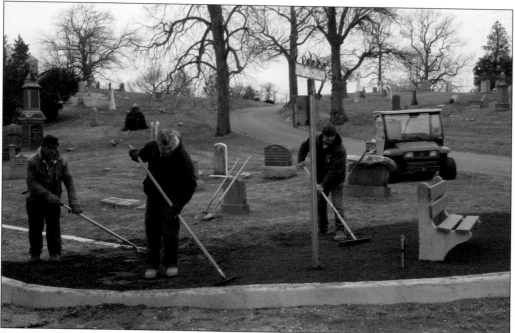

Cypress Hills has 27 dedicated field personnel who take great pride in their work. The average infield employee has at least 25 years experience. When visiting Cypress Hills, one cannot help but notice the close attention to detail of the landscape and the aesthetic continuity of stone with nature.

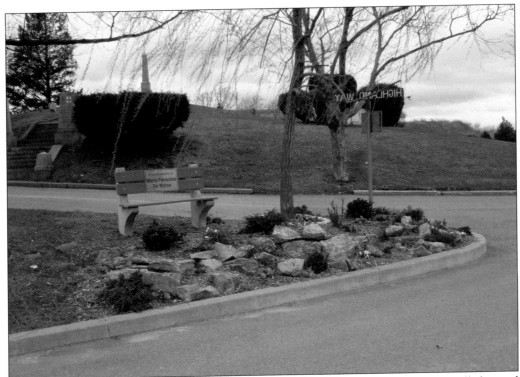

Another way to remember a loved one is sponsoring a Cypress Hills sitting bench, usually located at the intersection of cemetery roadways. This memorial bench is in loving memory of Maria Patrocinio De Matos. These benches beautify the cemetery and create a park-like atmosphere.

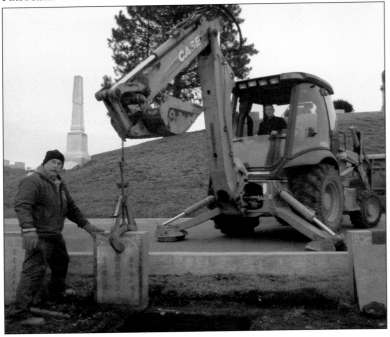

Field Operators take great care with stone monuments, for each stone represents a life lived. Daily, they must lift, move, and reposition headstones because of the ongoing grave digging operations. The clamping device that is attached to the stone tablet that easily lifts and lowers the stone is called "Monumental No-Hands." Both clamps have rubber ends to provide grip and protection to the precious stone.

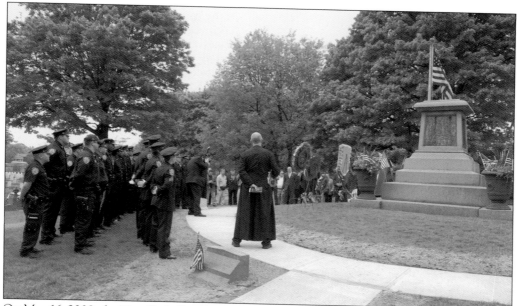

On May 16, 2008, the New York City Benevolent Police Association gathered for the first time in over half a century at the Police Arlington Memorial. The event was well attended with uniformed officers, NYPD brass, and other interested parties to honor the police officers buried here. They held a formal ceremony to renew their commitments to fully restore this important monument and to replace the statue of officer Lester Lewis that stood on the pedestal.

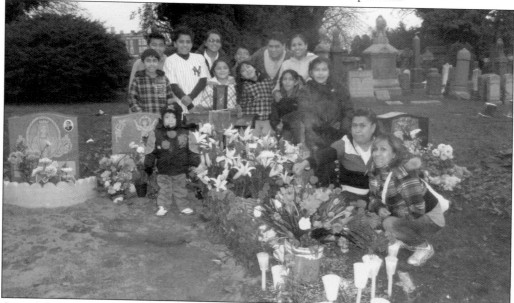

One of the most special and meaningful rituals is el Dia de los Muertos, or "the Day of the Dead." Celebrated in Mexico and in other Latin cultures, on November 2, the Day of the Dead is a time to happily and lovingly visit the grave site and remember departed relatives. Here a Mexican family in Cypress Hills celebrates over a loved one's highly decorated grave. This special day for the Latin culture is the equivalent of All Souls Day, which is also recognized on the same date.

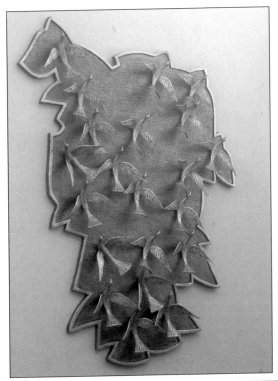

In the past few years Cypress Hills has invested time and a great deal of money in beautifying the grounds with art and sculptures. This bronze work at left depicts birds in flight, which graces the north face of the Melrose Memorial Garden mausoleum.

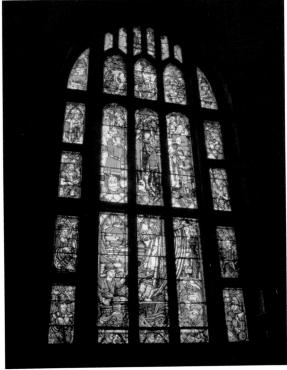

This magnificent two-story stained-glass window in the Memorial Abbey was recently restored due to the ravages of wind, rain, ice, and age, as it is 80 years old. The restoration project included replacing broken or cracked glass and deteriorated lead frames. Established in 1920, Rohlf's Stained and Leaded Glass Studio, Inc., was responsible for the complete restoration project.

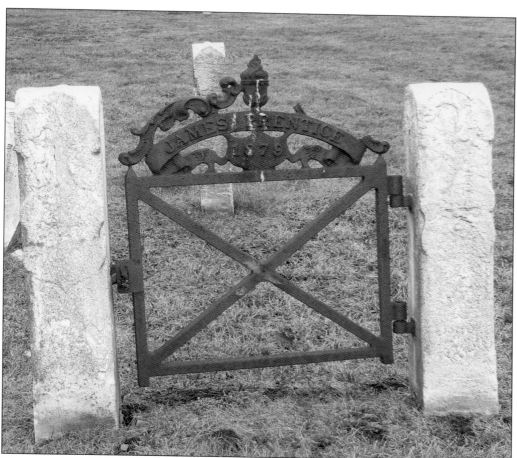

"A series of gates, from childhood to adulthood we must pass—then the next life's pearly gates open to us at last."

—Anonymous

www.arcadiapublishing.com

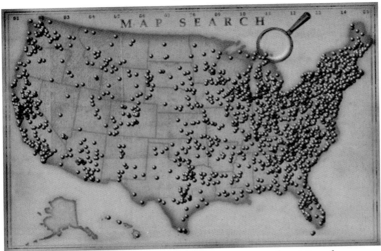

Discover books about the town where you grew up, the cities where your friends and families live, the town where your parents met, or even that retirement spot you've been dreaming about. Our Web site provides history lovers with exclusive deals, advanced notification about new titles, e-mail alerts of author events, and much more.

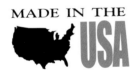

MADE IN THE USA

Arcadia Publishing, the leading local history publisher in the United States, is committed to making history accessible and meaningful through publishing books that celebrate and preserve the heritage of America's people and places. Consistent with our mission to preserve history on a local level, this book was printed in South Carolina on American-made paper and manufactured entirely in the United States.

This book carries the accredited Forest Stewardship Council (FSC) label and is printed on 100 percent FSC-certified paper. Products carrying the FSC label are independently certified to assure consumers that they come from forests that are managed to meet the social, economic, and ecological needs of present and future generations.

FSC
Mixed Sources
Product group from well-managed forests and other controlled sources

Cert no. SW-COC-001530
www.fsc.org
© 1996 Forest Stewardship Council

Find Your Place in History.